P9-DID-762

MODERN
NATIONS
—OF THE—
WORLD

SYRIA

BY TERRI DOUGHERTY

LUCENT
BOOKS®

THOMSON
─────✦─────™
GALE

San Diego • Detroit • New York • San Francisco • Cleveland • New Haven, Conn. • Waterville, Maine • London • Munich

On cover: Aleppo, Syria

LIBRARY OF CONGRESS CATALOGING-IN-PUBLICATION DATA

Dougherty, Terri
  Syria / by Terri Dougherty
    p. cm. — (Modern nations of the world series)
  Summary: Discusses the geography, history, people, and art of Syria, as well as the chal-
lenges the country is currently facing.
  Includes bibliographical references and index.
    ISBN 1-59018-246-4 (hardback : alk. paper)
    1. Syria—Juvenile literature. I. 1. Title. II. Series.
  DS93.D68 2004
  956.91—dc22

2004010200

CONTENTS

INTRODUCTION

Syria is a country steeped in antiquity. Located just east of the Mediterranean Sea, its position at the juncture of Europe, Asia, and Africa has made it an important trade route and highly sought-after piece of land since ancient times. It is the land of the biblical patriarchs, Roman city building, and battles between the crusaders and Muslim armies under Saladin, the Syrian military leader and ruler. However, Syria's place in world history is not only to be thought of in the past tense. It continues to shape the direction of history, as it plays an important role in the present-day politics of the Middle East.

Historically, the people of Syria have been merchants and traders. Syria forms a bridge of land between three continents, and Syrian cities grew up along trade routes as merchants found the route across Syria's rocky desert to be the best way to reach the Mediterranean Sea and Egypt's Nile River Valley. These regions were linked to the cultures of the East by these Syrian trade routes.

Syria's history has also been a tumultuous one. Its central location and the prosperity that came from its trade routes, fertile coast, and desert oases made it a highly desirable prize for the great empires of history. From ancient empires to Roman, Mongol, and Turkish armies, the world's conquerors have fought for control of Syria.

Syria has been shaped by its people and conquerors, and the remnants of the successive waves of rulers are still evident in the country's culture. From historic ruins of Roman amphitheaters to the predominance of the Muslim religion, the ideas and practices brought to the country over thousands of years have been melded into the culture of the nation that Syria is today.

MODERN SYRIA

While the nation's rich past is very much a part of present-day Syria, the nation today is also the product of more recent world events. Its current boundaries were drawn in the twentieth century, and it has been an independent nation since 1946. A relatively young independent country, it has struggled at times with self-government.

Syria is a predominantly Arab and Muslim nation, yet differences between social classes and various Muslim groups led to struggles for control and numerous changes in leadership early in the country's independent history. Syria's people identify more readily with their region of the country than with Syria as a whole. In addition, Syria's people retain religious and ethnic loyalties that stretch back centuries, and the relatively recent rise of independence has heightened these differences.

Political events in the Middle East have also had an impact on the modern nation of Syria. The creation of Israel in 1948 stirred resentment in Syria, and the two nations remain at odds. Syria also maintains influence over its neighbor Lebanon, and it has been accused of harboring terrorist groups. The actions of Syria's leaders can be surprising, however. Syria has traditionally shown a dislike for the West, and it disapproved of the U.S. war in Iraq in 2003, but supported the United States in the Gulf War in the early 1990s. With its

One of the oldest cities in the world, Damascus is Syria's capital and home to 5 million people.

ability to influence events in the Middle East, Syria remains a powerful player in world politics.

Syria's internal political structure is built on power as well. The rise of the Baath Party in the 1950s provided Syria with a dominant political organization. In power since 1963, its leaders have used an authoritarian—and sometimes brutal—style of government to keep the differences between Syria's various ethnic and religious factions from escalating to civil war, and to stifle opposition to the government.

Syria's president, Bashar al-Assad, and the Baath Party have been able to keep the fragmented nation from erupting into factional fighting by maintaining a firm hold on the country. Bashar al-Assad is a shrewd leader, as his father, Hafez al-Assad, was before him. However, Bashar al-Assad

A group of Syrian men demonstrates in Damascus against U.S. military involvement in Iraq. Syria strongly disapproves of U.S. involvement in the Middle East.

has shown some signs of being more lenient than his father was with regard to political freedom, and he also promised economic reform. His challenge is that he must work with a political structure that has been built on rewarding people with connections to the government, as well as lead a nation divided by ethnic and religious differences.

Syria is a country that must shape its future within the confines of its past. The people of Syria are proud of their traditions and their Arabic lineage, and the nation boasts a rich cultural heritage as well as intriguing archaeological finds. How Syria uses these cultural assets to its advantage will be for its leaders to decide.

1

FROM SEA TO DESERT

The Syrian Arab Republic, or Syria, is in a part of the world known as the Middle East. Located at the juncture of the European, Asian, and African continents, the Middle East has served as a crossroads, a meeting point, and a battleground for the world's many cultures for thousands of years. Syria's central location has placed it at the heart of great civilizations as well as major conflicts.

Syria has an area of 71,504 square miles, which is roughly the same size as North Dakota. To the north of Syria is Turkey, while Iraq is to its east and southeast. Jordan is south of Syria, and the Mediterranean Sea, Lebanon, and Israel border Syria to the west. A portion of Syria's land is in dispute: The Golan Heights, a region of about five hundred square miles, is occupied by Israel, although Syria still claims the area.

It is Syria's landscape rather than its politics that greatly influences where the majority of Syrians live. Two-thirds of the country's 17.6 million people live within seventy-five miles of the Mediterranean Sea. This western region of Syria includes the country's largest cities, Damascus and Aleppo. Most Syrians live in the western area because the eastern side of Syria's landscape is dominated by a rocky desert, and the climate is milder. In addition, the water supply is easier to come by.

CLIMATE

Most of Syria has a hot climate, but it varies from dry, hot, and windy in the desert to hot and humid on the Mediterranean coast. In July and August, temperatures in the desert regularly rise to more than 100 degrees, and often reach 110 degrees. The desert is arid and windy, and sandstorms can whip up during February and May. These storms can be so fierce that plants are damaged, and animals cannot graze.

Along the Mediterranean coast, the climate is humid in the summer, but the heat is not as intense as it is in the desert. Temperatures are usually in the 80s or 90s, and the heat is generally moderated by cool sea breezes. However, between May and September, the hot desert wind sometimes blows to the cities nearer the coast. In Syria's hills and mountains, the summertime weather is generally moderate and cloudy, with temperatures around 72 degrees.

Spring and autumn are the most pleasant seasons of the year in Syria. As one travel writer puts it, "Spring is when the country is at its greenest, the wild flowers and olive groves are in full blossom and the showers and cooler air mean that the atmosphere is free from haze, so you get the best views."[1] Between late March and early June, and again from early September to early November, temperatures are mild, generally 60 to 70 degrees.

Winter in Syria is cold and generally rainy along the coast and in the coastal mountains. Along the coast, the temperature ranges from the high 40s to the high 60s. There is snow in the higher elevations of the mountains in the winter, where the temperature hovers around the freezing mark. The temperature can also fall to freezing in Syria's plains and desert.

The Golan Heights, a region of nearly five hundred square miles in southwest Syria, has been occupied by Israeli forces since 1967. Syria, however, lays claim to the area.

Most of the country's rain falls between late October and May. The coastal areas can get as much as forty inches of rain a year, while the desert may get as little as four inches. The amount of rainfall varies from year to year; years of plentiful rainfall are often followed by periods of drought, when the desert may receive no precipitation.

THE SYRIAN DESERT

Two-thirds of Syria is covered by desert. The mountain range Jabal an Nusayriyah, which runs north and south along the coast, prevents significant rainfall from reaching the interior of the country. Although there are some fertile areas in the rocky desert region, much of the land east of the mountains is dry.

The Syrian Desert plateau slopes downward from the mountains in the west to the Euphrates River, the desert's eastern boundary. Although most of Syria's desert is rocky, there are some sandy areas in the north, along Syria's border with Iraq. Farther south, the desert gets rockier and more mountainous. In the southwest, the landscape is dotted with huge, black basalt boulders in the volcanic zone of the mountain range Jabal al Arab. Little vegetation can be found in the desert, although there are areas of scrub grass between the rocky regions. Tribes of nomadic herders, the Bedouin, raise sheep in the harsh environment, as they have done since ancient times. There are pockets of fertile areas in the desert, as rivers flowing from the mountains and underground springs feed desert oases. Palm trees growing in the oases offer shade, and the springs provide water for people and animals. The western part of the desert blooms in the spring, when moisture is most abundant.

The Euphrates River and its tributaries provide water for the fertile area east of the desert called the Jezira region. The Jezira is part of the Fertile Crescent, which reaches into Iraq and Turkey and was home to early civilizations such as the Babylonians, the Sumerians, and the Assyrians. Today, irrigation from the Euphrates River allows much of the region to be used for farming, as crops such as cotton are grown. The northeast corner of the Jezira region is also the source of Syria's main oil and natural gas resources, commodities which are valuable to the country's economy.

ANIMALS IN SYRIA

The people who lived in ancient Syria survived by hunting wild game and gathering food. Lions, wild bulls, and elephants were found on the Syrian plain, and civilizations such as the Assyrians hunted them for sport as well. However, the wild beasts, herds of antelope, and flocks of game birds that once enlivened Syria's landscape were hunted nearly to the point of extinction by the late 1800s and early 1900s. Some bears, antelope, deer, hyenas, and wildcats may still live in some of the more remote areas of the country, but Syria has no national parks, and it does not have a history of protecting wild species from overhunting.

Small, wild animals that live in Syria include foxes, badgers, and squirrels. Porcupines can also be found there, and the desert is home to snakes, lizards, and chameleons. Eagles and falcons still soar in the skies over Syria, while flamingos and pelicans inhabit the marshy areas on the edge of Syria's waterways.

A number of domesticated animals are important to Syria's agricultural communities. Nomadic herders keep flocks of sheep and goats, while camels and donkeys are used for travel. Lamb is an important source of meat, and goats' milk is made into cheese.

Domesticated animals like sheep and goats provide Syria's nomadic people with important sources of meat and milk.

THE COASTAL PLAIN

Along the coast of the Mediterranean, and to the west of the Jabal an Nusayriyah, lies the narrow coastal plain. It is heavily populated and intensely cultivated. The flat, fertile plain stretches more than seventy miles from Syria's Turkish border to Lebanon. It is about twenty miles wide at its widest point, and in some places it disappears as the Jabal an Nusayriyah meets the Mediterranean Sea. The plain is widest near Latakia in the north and Tartus in the south.

Reaching a height of nearly ten thousand feet, Syria's highest mountain peak, Mount Hermon, dominates the Syrian-Lebanese border.

The coastal plain boasts rich soil that has been cultivated for centuries. The slopes of the mountains receive moisture that is carried on a westerly wind blowing in from the Mediterranean Sea. The fertile region produces olives, tobacco, and fruit, and pine and oak trees grow in the northern part of the mountain range.

MOUNTAINS

South of the Jabal an Nusayriyah is a valley called Homs Gap. The valley lies between the Jabal an Nusayriyah and the Anti-Lebanon mountains to the south, and it is the easiest way to get from the Mediterranean Sea to the east. It has served as a trade route for centuries.

South of Homs Gap, the Anti-Lebanon mountains follow Syria's border with Lebanon. Mount Hermon, the highest mountain in Syria, is part of this chain. Reaching a height of 9,232 feet, it is on the Syrian-Lebanese border. Clusters of oak, pine, and cedar trees grow in these mountains, as well as cypress trees.

The slopes of Mount Hermon descend to the Hauran Plateau, which is able to get rain from Mediterranean winds and has areas of fertile soil. Areas of dark basalt and volcanic rock also dot the landscape of the region, which extends southward to the Jabal al Arab mountains along Syria's border with Jordan. On the southwest edge of the Hauran is the Golan Heights, Syria's disputed border with Israel.

Rivers

While Syria's mountain ranges define the country's rainfall patterns, three main rivers provide Syria with the valuable resource of water. The Euphrates in the northeast, the Orontes in the west, and the Barada in the southwest provide water for Syria's cities and farmland. In a hot, dry land, they provide a vital source for sustaining life.

The Euphrates River in northeastern Syria has supplied civilizations with a source of water since ancient times. It begins in Turkey, flows across Syria diagonally, and enters Iraq. The river is twenty-one hundred miles long and runs through Syria for about three hundred miles. The longest river in Syria, it provides 80 percent of Syria's water. Two tributaries flow into the Euphrates, the Balikh and the Khabur.

On the western side of the country, the Orontes River begins at Homs Gap and flows northward into Turkey through the Ghab Depression, which is also called the Great Rift Valley. Flowing on the eastern side of the Jabal an Nusayriyah mountains, it provides water for the cities of Homs and Hamah. Underground springs in the Ghab Depression also provide water for drinking and irrigation.

The Barada River is small but feeds the Al-Ghuta Oasis, the water source for Syria's capital city of Damascus. The Barada begins in the mountains and flows to the northeast, draining into a marshy area near the Damascus airport. It has brought water to Damascus for thousands of years, and an aqueduct built when the Romans ruled over the land continues to bring water to the city. In addition to supplying water for the people and industries of Damascus, the Barada also provides the area with water for apricot, peach, apple, and olive orchards. The groves are irrigated with well or river water in dry months.

Major Cities

Water is vital to life, and it is no accident that Syria's capital city grew up on a fertile oasis at the edge of a harsh desert. Damascus is located east of the Anti-Lebanon mountains, situated on the cusp of the Syrian Desert.

One of the oldest cities in the world, Damascus was settled as early as the fourth century B.C. In ancient times, merchants beginning their long trek across the desert stopped in Damascus for provisions. Traders coming from the east were able to find food, water, and a place to rest in Damascus after their long journey.

Damascus today reflects both the modern and the ancient, as its churches, mosques, and narrow streets recall the city's past. People still walk along the street called Straight, which the apostle Paul mentioned in the Bible's New Testament. The tomb of the Arabic leader Saladin is in Damascus, and merchants still sell goods in the markets, or souks. The city is not only known for its past, however. With 5 million people in the metro area, Damascus is Syria's largest city. It has modern apartment buildings and roads to accommodate the city's growing population.

In the northern part of Syria, the city of Aleppo depended on its location rather than water as its main resource. Resting on a plateau on the plains, the city provided its founders with a formidable defensive position from invaders. Emphasizing the city's defensive strength and dominating the city's skyline is the Citadel, built in the twelfth century on top of a natural mound in the center of the city. Its moat, bridge, and dramatic entrance gateway are a lasting reminder of the city's fortitude.

Founded around the same time as Damascus and now boasting a population of 4.5 million, Aleppo is the second-

THE FERTILE CRESCENT

The rich land along Syria's Mediterranean coast, north of the country, and along the Tigris and Euphrates rivers is known as the Fertile Crescent. The soil in the Fertile Crescent is so rich that some believe the Garden of Eden, the biblical home of Adam and Eve, was located in this region. This bow-shaped region was home to some of the world's earliest civilizations. The Sumerians were among the first to live in the area, as were the Babylonians, the Phoenicians, and the Hebrews. Because it was the birthplace of early cultures, it became known as the cradle of civilization.

The people living in the Fertile Crescent thrived because of the region's rich, cultivated farmlands. However, due to natural changes in the landscape, the water resources that once flowed into the region have been diminished, decreasing the amount of land available for farming.

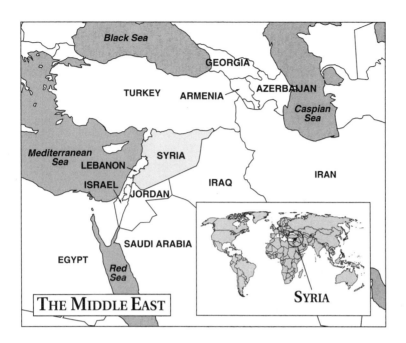

largest city in Syria. Like Damascus, the city operates much the way it has for centuries, with people trading in the busy covered markets and making their way through the maze of streets. Aleppo is home to a conservative Muslim population and to various Christian religious groups. One of Syria's most industrialized cities, its people produce machinery, woven silk, and cotton products. Aleppo's history includes periods of independence and connections with Europe, which blend with a religiously diverse population to give it a special character.

South of Aleppo is Hamah, one of Syria's most conservative cities. Many of the Muslims who live in Hamah are from the Sunni sect. Sunni Muslims make up the majority of Syria's Muslim population and are the largest division in Islam. They strictly follow orthodox ways, and many women wear traditional black veils. Like other cities in Syria, however, Hamah is also a mixture of the old and the new. Waterwheels from the Middle Ages still creak and turn with the flow of the Orontes River, and people rest in the gardens beside the river. Some of the city's past has been erased, however, as much of the city was damaged in 1982, during fighting between the government and local rebels. Since then the city has been engaged in rebuilding.

In the city of Hamah, a medieval waterwheel continues to operate. Hamah's predominately Sunni Muslim population relies heavily on traditional technologies.

South of Hamah is Homs, which is also on the Orontes River. Traders have gathered in Homs since ancient times but the people of this city are more interested in the present than in the past. Homs is an industrial center and is home to the country's largest oil refinery. It also is at the center of Syria's phosphate industry.

While Homs is one of Syria's most industrialized cities, Latakia is one of its most cosmopolitan. The main port in Syria, the city has a population of about 315,000 people. Influenced by the many cultures that engage in trade with the city, the community is the least conservative of Syria's cities. Women may wear clothing that is more Western in appearance than is seen in other Syrian cities. Latakia and the surrounding area is home to members of the Alawi religious community, a branch of Islam. Latakia has been in existence since 1000 B.C., when Phoenician fishermen settled there, and takes its name from the mother of a leader who ruled the region around 300 B.C. Over the course of the city's history, it has managed to survive earthquakes and invaders and has been at times a sleepy fishing village and at others a bustling port city. Under President Hafez al-Assad, who ruled Syria from 1970 to 2000, the city's harbor was redeveloped into the best port in Syria.

Tartus, south of Latakia, is Syria's second-largest port. Tartus and the island of Arwad near its coast have roots that can be traced to ancient times, when the city was established by the Phoenicians as a trading base. During the Crusades in the Middle Ages, when Christians and Muslims fought over the Holy Land, Tartus's location on the Mediterranean Sea was seen as a key strategic location. In the old sector of the city, the remains of a fortress used by the crusaders still stands.

Ruins of ancient buildings like the first-century temple dedicated to Baal, a native Syrian god, in the city of Palmyra provide tangible reminders of the country's remote past.

LINKS TO THE PAST

Structures such as the crusader fortress in Tartus are visible reminders of the centuries-old roots of Syria's cities. The cities are not the only places where Syria's past is evident,

however. Buried under the desert sand, and preserved by the dry climate, are the ruins of past civilizations. The tells, or artificial mounds, that rise from the landscape are often the remains of former civilizations that have been buried or built upon. In the Jezira region, portions of an ancient walled city can be seen rising from the desert. The remains of castles from the era of the Crusades in the Middle Ages rest in the Orontes Valley, including the impressive and well-preserved Krak des Chevaliers. Archaeologists examine these remains and ruins to gather more information about Syria's past. In doing so, they learn about some of the world's first civilizations from the secrets buried underneath Syria's shifting sands.

Learning about the past is important, as the remains of past civilizations are as much a part of Syria's landscape as its mountains and rivers. With access to the sea, passage through mountains, and oases that offer respite from the harsh desert, Syria's land has been coveted by the great civilizations of world history. With a landscape and a climate that are at times harsh and forbidding and at others inviting and nurturing, Syria has linked many cultures and nations, providing them with hope for the future as well as a bridge to the past.

CONQUERED BY THE GREAT EMPIRES OF HISTORY

2

Ancient Syria was at the center of early trade routes, and control of the region became a much sought-after prize for strong ancient empires. Syria's coastline offered a link to the Mediterranean Sea to the west, while passages through its mountains provided traders with access to the markets of the East. Control of this land was an opportunity for kings, emperors, and sultans to exert their influence well beyond their borders.

The area referred to as Greater Syria in ancient times was a much larger territory than present-day Syria. The region was bordered on the west by the Mediterranean Sea, the Taurus Mountains to the north, and the Arabian and Sinai deserts to the east and to the south. It included present-day Lebanon, Jordan, and Israel, as well as parts of Turkey and Iraq.

THE ANCIENT WORLD

Ancient Syria was home to some of the world's oldest civilizations. The first people living in Syria were nomadic hunters and gatherers who followed their prey. Eventually these nomadic tribes began settling in communities, and thus ancient Syria became the location of some of the first organized settlements.

People settled in villages that eventually became cities, such as Ebla in northern Syria, which was one of the first to dominate the region. To Ebla's east was Mesopotamia, the "cradle of civilization," where a powerful community grew up between the Tigris and Euphrates rivers. Here, the Babylonians developed a culture that advanced the arts and sciences.

19

EBLA

The city of Ebla, south of present-day Aleppo in northern Syria, was one of the first settlements to flex its power in the ancient world. Discovered by archaeologists in 1975, the city was the headquarters of an empire that reached from the Red Sea in the south to Turkey in the north between 2400 and 2300 B.C.

The estimated 260,000 people of Ebla spoke a Semitic language that is the oldest language of its type. From coastal seaports, its people traded with Egypt. They also sent goods through Syria to Mesopotamia. Ebla's power expanded as it conquered the cities of other civilizations such as Mari, the capital of the Amorite people on the southern part of the Euphrates River.

Ebla's power did not last, however. It was burned by a conquering nation around 2300 B.C. The Amorites, based in southern Iraq, took control of much of Syria, including Ebla. Artifacts from the ancient cities of Ebla, Mari, and Ugarit are on display in museums in Aleppo.

Pictured are ruins of the city of Ebla, the seat of an ancient Syrian empire.

On Syria's coast, trading communities were developing and doing a brisk business with Egypt. The Canaanites inhabited the coastal region. They intermarried with Syrians and their children became the Phoenicians. The seafaring Phoenicians built a powerful trading empire around 2000 B.C., and their civilization made great developments in building and communication. They developed iron tools and the alphabet and were renowned for their shipbuilding. They also created and organized a series of city-states that solidified their trading dominance.

COVETED REGION

Syria's strategic trading location, fertile soil, and stocks of timber along the coast made it a desirable possession for the major civilizations of the day. The country's many resources made it impossible for other nations to ignore it, and also made it difficult for its people to be independent. The people of Greater Syria were often under the control of other nations.

Around 1300 B.C., the Israelites, Hebrew people who believed in one God, migrated to the southern coast and hills. They were the world's first monotheistic people and introduced their beliefs to the region. King David, the second king of Israel, established the nation's capital at Jerusalem around 1000 B.C.

A relief sculpture depicts an Assyrian god. The Assyrians conquered Syria in the eighth century B.C.

The Israelites were often at war with the Aramaeans, who controlled the western part of Greater Syria. The capital of their country of Aram was in Damascus, and the Aramaeans dominated western Syria and established trade routes to southwest Asia. The Aramaic culture influenced the Middle East and Persian Empire, and remnants of the Aramaic civilization remain in Syria. For example, at Aleppo, an Aramaic fortress still stands, and the language of Aramaic is still spoken in some cities in Syria.

The entire region of Greater Syria was conquered by the Assyrian Empire in the eighth century B.C. Over the next several hundred years, the Babylonians, the Egyptians, and the Persians also had control of the region at various times. The influence of the Persian Empire remains in Syria's architecture. The Persians introduced an architectural style that used three-sided hallways covered by a curved ceiling. One side was left open and overlooked a courtyard. The style, called *iwan*, became popular throughout the region.

GREEK AND ROMAN EMPIRES

The Persian Empire was conquered by the Greek armies led by Alexander the Great in 333 B.C. After Alexander's death, his general, Seleucus, ruled Syria. The Greeks established settlements in Syria, such as Latakia on the coast of the Mediterranean Sea. The Greeks brought with them advances in science, art, and the philosophy of Aristotle. Their ideas were blended with Syrian learning, resulting in a mixture of Eastern and Western cultures.

The Romans overtook the Greek Empire, and Syria became a Roman province in 64 B.C. Spurred on by their location as trading centers, Syrian cities grew. The Romans introduced a tax system based on farmland harvests that remained in place for centuries, and their architecture, aqueducts, wells, and roads remain visible reminders of Roman rule over Syria. One of the Romans' agricultural projects was to develop olive groves in Aleppo, and the crop is still harvested there today.

The Roman emperor Constantine moved the capital of his empire from Rome to Byzantium, which he renamed Constantinople and is now called Istanbul in present-day Turkey. The Byzantine Christians built monasteries in Aleppo and Damascus, which still stand, and there are Christian communities in present-day Syria that have their roots in the Byzantine era.

The period of Byzantine rule, from 330 to 635, was an uneasy one. The country was constantly in conflict with the Persian Empire to the east, and warfare weakened the forces of both. Many of the people in the northern part of the country converted to Christianity and supported the Byzantine Empire, but those who lived in the south did not convert and were not loyal to the Byzantine leaders. When the Byzantines could no longer afford to support the Arabs living in Syria's steppe region, the people there came under the influence of Islam, which was moving into Syria from the Arabian Peninsula.

UMAYYAD MUSLIMS

While Syria has been touched by many cultures over the centuries, the event that has had the greatest impact upon the country has been the introduction of Islam. The roots of the Islamic religion go back to what is now Saudi Arabia in the year A.D. 570. In this area south of Syria, the prophet Muhammad began preaching in the streets of Mecca. He preached that revelations from the angel Gabriel had come to him, and he was commanded to teach others about a belief in Allah, the need to care for the poor, and the end of the world. His message was rejected in Mecca but accepted in other cities and villages of the Arabian Peninsula. The numbers of followers grew, and they zealously spread their beliefs.

Followers of the Muslim religion entered Syria in 636, and Damascus became the center of an empire overseen by Muslim leaders who brought the Arabic language to the region. Rulers from the Umayyad family led an empire that stretched from Spain, along the African coast, to Arabia and Iran. Syria prospered under the Umayyad Muslims, trading with foreign countries, building hospitals, and engineering water systems. Intellectuals came to Damascus to study medicine and philosophy, sharing their ideas and enriching the culture. Muslim leaders allowed those of other faiths to continue to practice their religions. The Muslim law, or sharia, applied to Arabs and Muslims, but non-Muslims were allowed to follow the laws dictated by their religion.

The Umayyads received pressure from other Muslim groups to the east, and a Muslim group called the Abbasids, based in Iran, took over Syria around 750. The capital of the empire was moved from Damascus to Baghdad in present-day Iraq, and Syria became a province of the empire.

THE CRUSADES

The power struggles within the Abbasid Empire weakened it and led to regions of Syria being separated into smaller states controlled by Muslim nobles. Some of these nobles made significant cultural contributions, particularly in the Aleppo region where poetry flourished. However, the region lacked political unity and was vulnerable to attack. In the late eleventh century, the Turks came into Syria from the northeast.

Their control extended into areas that Christians considered holy, and Christians did not want their ability to visit places such as Jerusalem and Bethlehem in the Holy Land in Palestine hampered by hostile tribes in the region. Protection for Christians traveling through Syria typically came from Western nations. When Muslim leaders tried to keep

Christians out of Jerusalem, soldiers called crusaders came from Europe to take the city.

Christian crusaders fought in Syria in the tenth and eleventh centuries. They gained control of Jerusalem and Damascus, built fortresses, and established seats of government along the coast. The fortress at Krak des Chevaliers is a sturdy reminder of the crusaders' presence. However, the Muslims were united in their hatred of these invading armies. This feeling of resentment would be carried through the centuries.

Damascus was taken back by Muslim armies and Saladin, a powerful leader from the Kurdish ethnic group, led an army that took Jerusalem from the crusaders in 1188. Saladin

KRAK DES CHEVALIERS

The wars between the crusaders and Muslim soldiers left a lasting impression on Syria's landscape. One of the most well-preserved examples of Syria's past is the crusaders castle Krak des Chevaliers, which still stands sturdily on a hilltop in western Syria. Thousands of knights once guarded the castle, which overlooks Homs Gap, an important trade route between the Mediterranean coast and major cities in Turkey and Lebanon.

The castle was fortified between 1150 and 1250, with a defensive system that included a moat and steeply sloping walls which prevented armies from climbing up. Openings in the roof allowed boiling oil to be poured onto enemies. Inside the castle were living quarters, including a great hall for banquets and meetings, kitchens, and a chapel.

After the crusaders left the castle, it was used for a time as a military base. Even after its importance as a military stronghold declined, it provided protection from the elements. Local peasants occupied the castle and lived in a village within its walls until the early 1900s.

Thousands of Crusaders once guarded Krak des Chevaliers, an imposing castle that still stands in western Syria.

united the area of Egypt and Syria under his rule and brought harmony to the Middle East, as Mulsims were proud of his military success and regional leaders came together under his leadership. His influence extended from the Tigris River in present-day Iraq to North Africa and the Sudan. However, after his death in 1192, control of the region was fractured by conflicts as various groups once again vied for power. Syria was now fragmented into smaller units of government.

Syria's fragmented government was no match for the conquering empires that came into the region from Central Asia and Egypt. Fierce Mongol warriors from Central Asia entered Syria, and in the early 1400s ravaged Aleppo and Damascus under the leadership of the warrior Tamerlane. Mongol armies in Syria clashed with the armies of the Mamluk sultans from Egypt. Despite repeated Mongol raids, the Mamluks established a hold on Syria and were able to put a unified system of government in place that oversaw trade and industry. Syria's importance as a center of trade, however, was on the verge of decline.

THE OTTOMAN EMPIRE

In 1498 a Portuguese explorer named Vasco da Gama found a water route around the horn of Africa. Traders began to ship goods overseas from the Far East to Europe, instead of taking an overland route. This impacted Syria's economy, as fewer trade caravans crossed its rocky desert. Repeated raids and sacking by Mongol warriors also ravaged the country, and Syria declined as Mamluk control of the region faltered.

The Ottomans—Muslim Turks who lived in Central Asia— began establishing a powerful empire around 1300 and competed with the Mamluks for control of the Middle East. The Ottoman sultan Selim I invaded Syria in 1516, and Mamluk control of its empire crumbled. The Ottomans ultimately gained control of almost all the Muslim world. The sultan's palace was located in Istanbul, Turkey, and Syria became a province of the empire.

The Ottomans, the last great empire to rule Syria, maintained control of the country for three hundred years. Their rule was not harsh toward obedient Syrians who followed the government and respected the governance of the pashas. The pashas were district leaders who had a great deal of authority over their regions. Common bonds between the people of

A page from a Turkish manuscript shows the coronation of Sultan Selim I, who took control of Syria in 1516.

Syria and their rulers made Ottoman rule tolerable. The Muslim religion was shared by many Syrians and the Ottoman administrators. Arabic, the language of both Syria and the Muslim holy book, the Koran, was respected by the Ottomans.

The Ottomans tolerated religions other than Islam, and religious groups such as Christians followed laws that were administered by their leaders. Britain, France, and Russia demanded that the Ottomans give them the right to oversee Christians living in Syria. This gave those countries a foothold in the Middle East, as they were able to exert some governmental influence over non-Muslim groups.

Although its citizens were not oppressed by the Ottoman rulers, Syria was no longer a rich nation. The reduction in trade goods flowing through the country that had begun in the early 1500s hurt its economy. Syria became a poor country for the most part, as inhabitants left and villages were abandoned. However, a few cities were still central trading points in the Middle East. Aleppo was a market town favored by European merchants. Spices, fruits, and textiles were traded in cities such as Sidon and Tripoli, which were part of Syria at that time. Damascus also held an esteemed position in Ottoman-ruled Syria, as pilgrims met there to begin their journey to the Saudi Arabian city of Mecca, a pilgrimage Muslims are required to make during their lifetime.

BEGINNING OF OTTOMAN DECLINE

Ottoman rule began to weaken in the 1700s. The pashas began fighting among themselves for control of land. The people of Syria were also hurt by the taxation system, which allowed landowners and tax collectors to profit at the expense of the peasants. Ahmad Pasha, the pasha who ruled over the areas of Sidon and Damascus in the late 1700s, was an example of both the good and the bad in the Ottoman system of government. An able administrator and a brave soldier who oversaw the building of a mosque, a library, and a fountain, he could also be a cruel and ruthless leader, as he heavily taxed the people and took over their land.

EGYPTIAN OCCUPATION

The Ottoman Empire faced threats from both within and without. France went to war with the empire, and Napoléon's army briefly controlled Syria's coast. Syria also came under attack from Egypt, which invaded the country in the 1830s looking for raw materials to use for its military. European nations helped the Ottomans push the Egyptians out of the country by 1839.

RULE OF THE PASHAS

Under the rule of the Ottomans, Syria was divided into four provinces, each administered by a pasha, the highest-ranking civil or military official in the province. Each province contained a capital city that was a center for the local economy. Islamic law was enforced for those who followed the Muslim religion, and men who were experts in the Islamic law, or sharia, were the governor's advisers. A *qadi* was the judge of the Muslim community and made decisions based on Islamic law. He had control over morality and schools, as well as economic issues such as the markets and weights and measures.

The pashas held a great deal of authority and could collect taxes from the people of their provinces. These high-ranking officials did not always treat the people fairly. In addition, the pashas often had their own ideas about how to govern their provinces and did not always get along with each other or the sultan, the sovereign ruler of the empire. The jockeying for power among these leaders weakened the Ottoman Empire.

Although Egyptian rule over Syria was brief, the Egyptians did make improvements to the government system, which were kept in place after their rule ended. The administrative system under the pashas was replaced by a more centralized system of governors who received a salary paid by the government. A stricter system of law and order was put in place under the Egyptians. Tribes that had forced travelers in the desert to pay for protection or risk being attacked as they traveled were punished.

This new system did not sit well with the old landowners who had profited from extracting taxes from the peasants under the old Ottoman system. Groups such as the Druze, a Muslim religious sect, had remained fairly autonomous during Ottoman rule and did not want additional oversight. There was also a growing resentment against Christian and Jewish businesspeople who had established trade agreements with European nations. This instability resulted in conflicts between Druze and Christian groups, and in 1860 thousands of Maronite Christians, members of a sect named after a fifth-century Syrian monk, were killed in a clash in southern Syria. The Druze were forced to flee to the Hauran area of Syria, and the Ottomans created Lebanon in southern Syria as a home for the Christians.

OTTOMAN DEFEAT

As Syrians became more dissatisfied with Ottoman rule, the idea of independence began to circulate among Syrians. Ottoman rulers such as the oppressive sultan Abdul Hamid II, who ruled the empire from 1876 to 1909, encouraged Syrians to consider ruling themselves. Secret societies were formed that favored independence, but Hamid did what he could to stop the independence movement, using spies, press censorship, and the death of opponents to maintain a grip on the empire. Successive leaders also tried to put an end to Syrians' ideas of independence. On May 6, 1916, the government had twenty-one Arabs hung in Damascus and Beirut for their part in independence movements. In their memory, May 6 is set aside each year as Martyr's Day and is a national holiday in Syria and Lebanon.

As the independence movement grew, the Ottoman Empire entered into World War I on the side of Germany, against France, Great Britain, and Russia. The war brought hope to

Syrians that they would have an independent nation after the war, and Great Britain courted Syrians who desired freedom from the Turks. They encouraged the Arabs to rebel against Ottoman rule and hinted that Syria would be independent and have an Arab leader after the war if England prevailed.

In 1918 Arab troops took control of Damascus, with guidance from British officers such as T.E. Lawrence, also called Lawrence of Arabia. After the war ended, Syrians organized a government and elected Prince Faisal ibn Hussein, the son of an influential Arab family and a military leader, as the country's king. He was appointed king of Syria, and worked to build it into a cohesive nation. He proclaimed Arabic as the official language of the country, replacing Turkish. Syrian leaders began organizing a system of education and writing a constitution. However, their self-government was short-lived.

Faisal ibn Hussein (front) ruled as king of Syria from 1918 until 1920, when France stationed troops in Syria and established a colonial government.

French officers in Damascus salute as the French national anthem is played. The French maintained control of Syria until the United Nations ordered an end to French rule in 1946.

The fate of Syria had been sealed several years before the war ended. In 1916 the Sykes-Picot Agreement was secretly drawn up, giving France influence in Syria and Lebanon, and allowing England to dominate Iraq and Transjordan, later called Jordan. The agreement was kept quiet until after the war, when the League of Nations officially gave France and Britain power to oversee these Middle Eastern nations. Syria was ruled by France under the French mandate. King Faisal ibn Hussein left Syria for Europe, and in 1921 was made king of Iraq by the British.

FRENCH RULE

Under the mandate established by the League of Nations, Syria would ultimately become an independent nation. However, Syrians were not happy with a promise of eventual independence. They did not want to be under French rule, and there was open rebellion against the French.

As France sought to maintain control over the region, it stationed troops in Damascus and Beirut. Newspapers, political activity, and civil rights were suppressed. Syrians' hatred of the French government at the time escalated into violence, and the French used artillery and troops to put down uprisings. Various groups were formed to support Syrian nationalism, and Syrians and the French worked out the Syrian-French treaty in 1936, which granted Syria independence. However, the document was never ratified by the French parliament.

REVOLTS AGAINST THE FRENCH

Although the Syrians resented the French influence over the way Syria was governed, life in general was improving under French rule. Damascus and Aleppo became modern cities, and roads and schools were built. Tribes that were persecuted in other nations, such as the Kurds, Armenians, and Assyrians, found refuge in Syria.

Life was not stable, however, as Syria had problems with Turkey. In 1939 France allowed the northwestern province of Alexandretta, which was then part of Syria but had a large Turkish population, to become part of Turkey. Syria felt it had not been fairly represented on the issue, and more unrest followed this decision.

French leader General Charles de Gaulle promised Syria that it would eventually gain independence. However, Germany took control of France during World War II and established a government at Vichy. In order to keep Germany from gaining control of French-held Syria, French and British forces entered the country in 1941. Syria came under Allied control during the war.

Syrians began to form their own government during the war. In 1943 a president was elected, and Syria's government took over control of some administrative affairs such as taxes and supervision of tribes. The United States, the Soviet Union, and Great Britain recognized Syria and Lebanon as sovereign states over the next few years, although France still did not want to give up control of the country and went as far as to use bombs to stop demonstrations in Damascus and Aleppo. The fighting ended after Great Britain's Winston Churchill threatened to support Syria. The United Nations ordered France to leave in 1946, and French rule ended on April 17, a date celebrated each year in Syria as Evacuation Day.

After centuries of rule by foreign powers, Syrians finally had a government of their own. The nation had been dominated by empires from the Greeks and Romans to the Ottomans and at last had a chance to assert its independence. The people of Syria had the opportunity to serve their own interests, rather than serving a foreign power. Freedom brought a new set of challenges to the nation, however. The people of Syria had been united in their desire to gain independence but now had to decide how to maintain that unity.

3 INDEPENDENT SYRIA

After the French left Syria, the nation's people were faced with the problem of finding the best way to govern the country. The people had been unified in their dislike of the French, but were otherwise more loyal to their religious faith or ethnic background than to Syria; people thought of themselves as part of the Muslim or Christian religion or the Kurdish or Bedouin ethnic group rather than as part of Syria. There were also divisions between the wealthy and the poor and between city dwellers and those who lived in rural areas.

There was also disagreement over how Syria's borders should be defined. Some Syrians thought the country should be part of a larger Arab state and thought of the true Syria as the Greater Syria of the ancient world, which had contained Lebanon, Jordan, and Palestine. Others thought Iraq or Egypt should influence how the country was governed. There was also support for a more independent Syria, strengthened by an alliance with the Soviet Union.

RESENTMENT AGAINST ISRAEL

Following World War II, a strong Arab unity movement swept through the Middle East. The Arab nations resented the creation of Jewish Israel, and the Western nations that supported that country. This sentiment was very evident in Syria. Syria viewed the region as Arab, and thus Muslim, territory, and there were demonstrations in Syria when the nation of Israel was created. Syria joined other Arab nations in war against Israel in 1948.

The Arab states lost the war, and this discredited Syria's leaders. Shukri al-Quwwatli, who had been elected president of Syria during World War II, was ousted by a military coup in 1949. The country's leadership was far from stable. The presidency changed hands two more times that year as coups rocked the country's government.

ARAB UNITY

The coup that took al-Quwwatli out of office was staged by Brigadier General Husni as Zaim, the army chief of staff. He lasted less than five months in office before he was ousted in a coup led by Brigadier General Sami al Hinnawi. Following the coup, Zaim was arrested and executed after a trial before the Council of War. Hashim Atassi, who had served as Syria's leader when the country was seeking independence from France, became president.

The government lasted only a few months before Colonel Adib Shishaqli took over. Shishaqli controlled Syria as a dictator from late 1949 until 1954. Under his guidance public works projects such as roads and hospitals were built. The Euphrates River project, which brought water to Aleppo, was begun. However, the military leader also ruled in an oppressive manner that curtailed the rights of the people. Shishaqli

★ ★ SYRIA'S FLAG

Syria's flag has undergone several changes since the country gained its independence from the Ottoman Empire in 1918. The country's first flag used the colors of the pan-Arab movement, black, green, white, and red. The white, green, and black colors stood for three Muslim dynasties that had ruled in the Middle East during the seventh through eleventh centuries, while red stood for the blood of martyrs. A triangle of red was on the left side of the first Syrian flag, with black, green and white stripes to its right.

During the time of the French mandate, the flag of Syrian independence was replaced with a banner that incorporated the French flag into the upper left-hand corner of the design. The pan-Arab colors were removed, and a blue background with a white circle was used until the Syrian revolt of 1925. The blue background was then replaced with two green stripes separated by a white band.

After the removal of French troops, Syria used several flag designs incorporating the pan-Arab colors of red, white, green, and black. Today's Syrian flag, adopted in the early 1980s, uses three boldly colored bars running horizontally across the flag. The top bar is red, the middle is white, and the bottom is black. Today the red color symbolizes how Syrians struggled and sacrificed to gain freedom, the white band stands for peace, and the black band stands for the nation's colonial past. Inside the white band are two green, five-pointed stars, which originally stood for unity with Egypt when the nation was aligned with Egypt in the United Arab Republic. The stars are now said to stand for unity between Syria and Iraq.

was removed from office by another coup, and the country
returned to civilian leadership when the government of
Atassi was restored.

The idea of pan-Arab unity was gaining popularity in Syria
at this time. This movement favored solidarity among Arab
regions. One of the strong advocates of pan-Arab unity was
the Baath political party, which attracted members in Iraq,
Lebanon, and Jordan in addition to Syria. The party contained people from all social classes who favored a united
Arab region but was especially popular with people from
Syria's poorer classes. They were tired of being oppressed by
wealthy landowners and felt empowered by the Baath Party's
advocacy of an even distribution of Syria's land and wealth.

In 1957 members of the Baath Party gained control of
Syria's government and, in the spirit of pan-Arab unity,

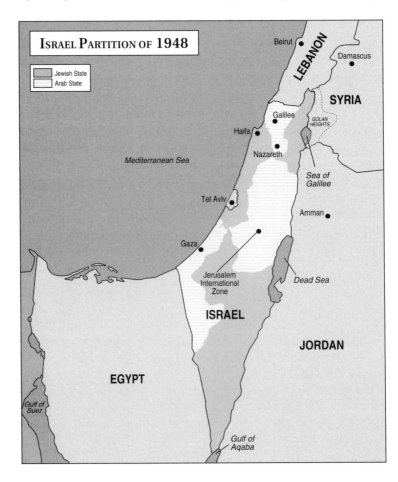

In 1958 Syrian president Shukri al-Quwwatli (right) holds hands with Egyptian president Gamal Abdel Nasser to celebrate the newly formed United Arab Republic. The union lasted only three years.

formed an alliance with Egypt. Syria's leaders also felt that joining with Egypt would strengthen their hold on Syria's government and give the country more stability. Not all Syrians favored the policies advocated by the Baath Party, however, and there were regional conflicts and disagreements between those who favored Socialist reforms and the wealthy urban merchants and landowners who wanted to maintain their power.

Syria and Egypt were joined in 1958 and became the United Arab Republic, with Gamal Abdel Nasser of Egypt as president. However, the union did not work out as Syria's leaders had hoped. Egypt dominated Syria's interests, and the unity ended in 1961.

STRUGGLES

After the unity with Egypt dissolved, Syrian army officers took over the government, with Nazim al-Qudsi as president. Syria's leadership changed hands several times in the early 1960s, and in 1963, Baath Party members gained control. The members were mainly from rural areas or villages, who had grown up in poor regions of the country. Outside of military service, they had few options for raising their social and economic status. Many had joined Syria's military in the 1950s, had risen through the ranks, and were now in positions of power in the military. A great number of these leaders were Alawis, a sect of the Muslim religion that is found mainly in the Syrian provinces of Latakia and Tartus. The Alawis traditionally were poor farmers who worked land owned by wealthy Sunni Muslims. Through military service, however, they gained power and prestige. In the new government leadership, they flexed their clout. This new power structure did not sit well with the Sunni Muslims, who had traditionally held political sway in the country.

While Baath Party members held on to the top government positions in Syria, there was still division within the party as to how the nation should be governed. Some members were in favor of Arab unity, such as the union with Egypt, while others wanted Syria to be more independent. Some advocated more government ownership of industry and land, in line with the party's Socialist beliefs. Eventually, the younger members of the party, who favored more Socialist policies than their more conservative counterparts, gained control in 1966. Salah Jadid directed government affairs as the leader of the Baath Party, and Nureddin Atassi was named president. The top government officials in the previous regime were arrested or left the country. The minister of defense in the new regime was Major General Hafez al-Assad, who would play a critical role in Syria's politics for the rest of the century.

AL-ASSAD TAKES POWER

Salah Jadid and Hafez al-Assad were both members of the Baath Party, but they did not share the same view of how Syria should be governed. Al-Assad was an army general who favored more moderate policies, while Jadid was a civilian with extreme views. At the same time Syria's government was

struggling with these leadership issues, it was also preparing
to join other Arab nations in an attack on its neighbor, Israel.
Syria continued to view Israel as Arab territory, and in 1967
it joined with Jordan and Egypt in a war against Israel.

Syria, Egypt, and Jordan were convinced that their military
power was superior to that of the Israeli army. The war, which
lasted only six days, proved otherwise. Syria's army per-
formed poorly, and half of its air force was destroyed. Israel

HAFEZ AL-ASSAD

Hafez al-Assad was born in 1930 in the village of Al-Qardahah
in the Latakia province of northwestern Syria. He was educated at the Syrian
Military Academy in Homs and the Air Force Academy in Aleppo. In 1946 he
became a member of the Baath Party to show his support for Syria's independence. He was a top combat pilot and a natural leader, becoming
squadron commander in 1957 and receiving training from the Soviet Union.

Al-Assad's connections in the Baath Party helped him obtain a post as the
leader of the Baathist Military Committee in Egypt during Syria's short-lived
union with Egypt in the United Arab Republic. After the union was dissolved
in a military coup and a non-Baathist government took power, al-Assad was
briefly jailed because of his political connections to the Baath Party. He was
released and given a low-level job in Syria. However, when the Baath Party
took over the government in 1963, al-Assad was able to rise through the
ranks in Syria's air force. He became the leader of the Ministry of Defense in
1966 and took control of the government in 1970.

Al-Assad was a calculating leader, who could coldly and shrewdly dis-
cern how to stay in power. He kept a grip on Syria and a strong role in the
Middle East by using terrorist groups as a type of secret weapon. He allowed terrorist groups to have bases in Syria, and by having some degree of
influence and control over them, he had a trump card to play when dealing
with other countries. He also used the terrorist groups to repeatedly punish
Israel for not returning the Golan Heights. Al-Assad dominated the leadership in Lebanon, a country that had been torn apart by civil war, by sending
troops to Lebanon to support the country's leadership. Through his support, al-Assad controlled the nation as a puppet state.

Some of al-Assad's moves were contradictory, however. He harshly suppressed fundamentalist opposition to his rule, as evidenced by the thousands killed in Hamah in 1982. However, he supported militant groups with
fundamentalist views, such as the Hizballah militia in southern Lebanon
and the Palestinian group Islamic Jihad, because they helped Syria in its ongoing conflict with Israel. Al-Assad played a dangerous game but was able to
keep the opposition in check and maintain his hold on Syria.

prevailed, and Syria lost control of the Golan Heights. This high ground had been an important strategic military position for Syria, which had used it to rain down bombs on Israel. The loss of this piece of land would remain a point of contention for decades, and would divide Syrian politics, as leaders blamed each other for the defeat.

Al-Assad and Jadid continued to disagree over the direction of Syria's leadership, and al-Assad eventually gained the military support he needed to take control of Syria. In November 1970, Jadid was arrested by army officials. The coup put al-Assad in power.

A SHREWD POLITICIAN

Hafez al-Assad quickly moved to solidify his grip on Syria's leadership. He had taken control of the Baath Party in 1970 and became president of Syria in 1971. He was the only candidate in the election, receiving 99.2 percent of the vote. His overwhelming win in the election did not reflect the true feelings of the Syrian people, however, as support for al-Assad was not universal. The vote instead reflected the inability of the people of the country to truly have a say in how they were governed.

Al-Assad took over a country of people with divided loyalties, but he was a shrewd politician who would use a mixture of political savvy and brute force to keep control over Syria. He knew that in order to maintain power he needed to show some tolerance for the country's varied religious and ethnic groups. In order to gain broader support, he created the People's Council. This gave some members of other political parties a voice in government, and helped quiet their dissatisfaction with al-Assad's domineering rule. The majority of the members of the People's Council belonged to the Baath Party, however.

A 1973 constitution supported by al-Assad gave him a great deal of power over Syria, but it also contained measures that were designed to pacify his opponents. Sunni Muslims, who represented the majority of Muslims in Syria, had traditionally held positions of wealth and political power. Al-Assad, however, was an Alawi. The Sunni Muslims resented the amount of powerful positions held by Alawis and also favored a more religiously centered government. They rioted to make their point.

In order to satisfy the Sunni Muslims, al-Assad supported the constitutional requirement that Islamic law be the basis of legislation in Syria. The constitution also decreed that the president of the country had to be Muslim. However, this decree had another impact. It implied that Alawis, like al-Assad were truly Muslim, although many Sunni Muslims and those from the Shiite Muslim sect, the second largest Muslim sect, regarded the Alawis as heretical. They did not believe that the Alawis followed accepted Muslim beliefs.

Al-Assad made it clear that he was in control of Syria, but he was neither a radical Socialist in favor of bringing more of Syria's economy under government control nor a staunch conservative with strict views on religion. He moved Syria's politics back toward the center of these two extremes.

Gaining the support of other Arab nations, as well as the Soviet Union, was also part of al-Assad's strategy. Syria did not have the vast oil reserves of other Middle Eastern nations and relied on money from other countries to support its military and its government budget. Other Middle Eastern nations gave aid to Syria, in return for Syria's continued support of anti-Israeli actions.

YOM KIPPUR WAR

The funds Syria received from Middle Eastern nations were used to improve its military equipment and training. In 1973, Egypt and Syria again attacked Israel. The war began on Yom Kippur, a Jewish holy day, and Syria again fought Israel over the Golan Heights. Syria initially succeeded in taking over some of its former land, but Israel retaliated and regained control. Syria lost even more land, and the war ended a few weeks after it began with no clear victor. In negotiations that followed the war, Israel agreed to partially withdraw from some Syrian territory. Syria was allowed to take back the land it lost during the war, as well as part of the Golan Heights.

CONFLICT IN LEBANON

Another area of conflict emerged near Syria as Christian and Muslim groups fought in Lebanon. Syria had an interest in Lebanon's politics, as Lebanon had traditionally been part of Syria. When Lebanon's Christians and Muslims entered into civil war in 1975, President Hafez al-Assad and Syria intervened on the side of the Christians. Al-Assad did not want

Israeli armored cars roll across the Golan Heights during the 1973 Yom Kippur War. With Egypt's help, Syria attacked Israel in order to regain control of the region.

the Muslim Palestine Liberation Organization to take over the country because he feared that Israel would retaliate. Syria sent troops to Lebanon in 1976, and a cease-fire was declared in the country's civil war.

Siding with the Christian forces against Palestinians and Muslims did not make Syria popular with other Arab nations. They were angered at Syria's position, which went against the pan-Arab unity movement. Syria, however, kept its troops in Lebanon in order to stay in control of the political situation there.

Syria's support of the Christian government was motivated by political rather than religious or pan-Arab motives. Syria wanted Lebanon to have a government that supported Syria and kept Lebanon's Christian leadership under tight control. When Tony Franjiyah, a Christian leader in Lebanon and supporter of Syria, was killed in 1978 by another member of the Christian group, Syria switched its support to the Muslim and Palestinian factions in the country. Christians came under attack from the Syrian military, and Syria continued to keep a hold on Lebanon with its military presence.

INTERNAL CONFLICT

The cost of keeping a military presence in Lebanon began to wear on Syria by the late 1970s. The country had benefited from economic aid from other Arab states, which had more oil resources and income than Syria did. However, after Syria sided with the Christian movement in Lebanon, the aid was reduced, and a major source of income for Syria became uncertain. Syria's economy suffered as it funneled money into its military, although a strong relationship with the Soviet Union brought in weapons and military advisers from that nation. However, this was not enough to quell a rising discontent within Syria.

In the early 1980s, the country's divisiveness began to intensify. Sunni Muslims were opposed to al-Assad, and they formed militant groups such as the Muslim Brotherhood. Al-Assad's opponents began to demand more freedom of the press, fair election, and less-restrictive political oversight.

Al-Assad felt that the only way to keep the country's religious factions from competing for power was to completely dominate them and to maintain strict control over the country. He filled government offices and police forces with those who shared his religious background or were related to him. Groups such as the Muslim Brotherhood used bombings and assassinations to try to reduce the power of al-Assad and

★ ★ THE ALAWI

Hafez al-Assad was a member of the Alawi religious sect, a branch of the Shiite Islamic sect. Many of the Alawi beliefs are secret and not readily shared with outsiders. Some of the Alawi rituals seem very unusual for the Muslim faith, such as celebrating the Christian holidays of Christmas and Easter and using bread and wine in religious ceremonies. Many Muslims of other sects view the Alawi religion as heretical.

The basic principles of the Alawi religion were formed in the ninth century. Although they were one of the poorest religious groups in Syria and were persecuted from the time of the Crusades through the end of Ottoman rule, their place in society was elevated when the French saw them as potential allies. In succeeding years, many Alawis entered the country's military and rose through the ranks. Members of the Alawi sect now wield considerable influence in Syria. Although about 12 percent of the country's population is Alawi, they dominate government offices and have political power that is out of proportion to their numbers. The country has been under Alawi leadership since 1971, and the Alawis have enjoyed the benefits of sharing the religion of the country's ruler.

other Alawi leaders in government. Hundreds were killed between 1976 and the early 1980s.

Strikes and riots broke out, mainly in Aleppo and Hamah, where many Sunni Muslims lived. Al-Assad decided to use even stronger action against the uprising. Military forces were sent to stop the unrest, and in 1982 the city of Hamah was virtually destroyed as aircraft and artillery rained down on the city, battering its buildings and killing its inhabitants. More than ten thousand people were killed in the clash, including one thousand soldiers.

STAYING IN CONTROL

Al-Assad was holding on to his position of power, thanks to his command of a secret police force and several military groups that acted outside of the command of Syria's regular military. However, in 1983 health problems almost cost him the presidency. He had a heart attack, which led to speculation that he was not in proper physical condition to run the country. Others saw this as an opportunity to make a bid for power.

One of those who thought he could take over was al-Assad's brother. Rifat al-Assad had been in charge of one of al-Assad's military groups and had helped keep his brother in power. Now, however, he wanted to take control for himself. Although he was ill, al-Assad garnered enough support to suppress the opposition to his leadership, and Rifat went into exile.

THE GULF WAR

Al-Assad was a shrewd leader who knew how to keep a tight grip on the government of his country. He also knew how to handle diplomacy with other nations. He did not hesitate to make a deal with nations once considered to be Syria's enemies when he saw it to be in Syria's best interest.

When Iraq invaded Kuwait in 1990, Syria was the first Arab state to condemn Iraq's action, and it sided with the United States in the Gulf War. Syria sent troops to defend Saudi Arabia from possible attack during the war, although Syria had traditionally distrusted the Western nations it was now allied with. However, Syria was also an enemy of Iraq and al-Assad decided that it would be better for Syria to set aside its differences with the United States in order to put down an old enemy.

A Syrian soldier stands guard next to the Syrian flag during the Gulf War. Syria was the first Arab nation to condemn Iraq's invasion of Kuwait.

TERRORIST LINK

Although Syria formed an alliance with the United States during the war, this did not mean that the United States agreed with al-Assad's leadership methods. Syria had strong ties to terrorist groups that inflicted violence and destruction on Israel, and the United States continued to denounce Syria's links with terrorist groups. Syria remained on the international list of countries that were supportive of terrorist groups.

Being labeled as a nation that supported terrorist groups impacted the amount of trade Syria was allowed to do with some nations. Housing the terrorist groups gave Syria some degree of control over them, however, and also provided Syria with a source of income. Wealthier Middle Eastern nations that supported the terrorist movements funneled money into Syria, and Syria was not about to give up the power or the money that the terrorist bases gave it.

AL-ASSAD'S LEGACY

Although he allowed Syria to maintain a connection to terrorist groups and ruled his country as a virtual dictator, al-Assad had provided Syria with stability. He did not want stability to be his only legacy, however. His health was failing him and as the end of his life neared, he desired to leave something more. He wanted to leave a legacy as a leader who enhanced Syria's position in the Middle East.

To do this, he decided to enter into peace talks with Syria's longtime enemy, Israel. Al-Assad had not supported

BASHAR'S RULE

At first it appeared that the British-educated Bashar al-Assad would ease some of the political restrictions his father had placed on the country. For instance, he released political prisoners and allowed political groups some freedom of the press, and thousands of Syrian troops were withdrawn from Beirut, although Syria did keep some soldiers in Lebanon.

Although it maintained its terrorist bases and anti-Israeli position, Syria provided information to the United States about al-Qaeda terrorists after the attacks in New York and Washington, D.C., on September 11, 2001. Syria had a wealth of knowledge about the location of terrorist leaders, as it had been tracking them around the world since its 1982 crushing of militant fundamentalist leaders in the Syrian city of Hamah.

Although Bashar al-Assad runs a less-authoritarian form of government than his father, rights such as free speech are still restricted. Powerful members of the Baath Party continue to influence how Syria is governed, and the freedom to oppose the government remains suppressed. Bashar al-Assad faces the same challenges as his father did, as he works to hold together a country where political rivalries run along religious lines and maintaining order means stifling the opposition. He must balance the need for stability with the rights of Syria's citizens. Whether he will be able to do it in a more peaceful and democratic manner than his father remains to be seen.

Although President Bashar al-Assad has eased some political restrictions in Syria, the basic civil rights of most Syrians are not guaranteed.

the Israel–Palestinian peace talks in the 1990s, which had provided for cooperation between Israel and Palestine and had given the Palestinians more self-government. He had also been opposed when Israel and Turkey had begun to strengthen their ties. However, he now felt that the time was right for him to try to add this achievement to his tenure as Syria's leader.

Through negotiations with Israel in late 1999 and early 2000, al-Assad tried to reach an agreement that would place the Golan Heights under Syrian control. Syria had lost control of this land to Israel in the 1967 war and felt that the entire Golan Heights should be returned to Syria. Israel would not withdraw from the Golan Heights, and the talks broke down in January 2000. Al-Assad had brought stability to Syria, but he would not be able to bring peace.

PASSAGE OF POWER

Al-Assad's health was failing, and he realized he would not be able to govern Syria for many more years. However, he wanted his family to maintain control of the country. His oldest son, Basil, had been groomed to take over leadership of the country from his father. However, after Basil was killed in a car accident in 1994, al-Assad looked to his younger son, Bashar, as his successor.

Not everyone agreed with al-Assad's choice. His brother, Rifat, still held out hope that he would one day rule Syria, and he and his supporters tried to gain a foothold in Syria by taking control of a port in Latakia. Their plan did not work, however, and his supporters were arrested and killed as al-Assad put down the uprising.

Al-Assad was firm in his choice of successor. Bashar, who had been trained in Great Britain as a physician, entered the Syrian military and quickly rose through the ranks. With his father's support, he was a colonel by 1999.

After several years of poor health, al-Assad died in June 2000. As he had planned, his son took over as leader of Syria. A law that set the minimum age for president at forty was conveniently lowered to thirty-four, Bashar al-Assad's age at the time he took control of the country. Bashar also became commander in chief of the armed forces and the leader of the Baath Party. In mid-July 2000, he was elected president with 97 percent of the vote.

4

GOVERNMENT SYSTEM

Bashar al-Assad governs Syria within a framework of government that is influenced by the many cultures that have inhabited Syria over the centuries. Syria's leaders, and especially Bashar al-Assad, have strict control over the way the country is run, but both the country's remote and recent past also influence the way it is governed. Some of the country's government practices date back to the time of Umayyad control, while other policies were developed more recently as the nation's leadership dealt with turmoil from within the country and pressure from other nations.

Syria's ethnic groups and the Muslim religion also play a role in the way the nation is governed. A fear that opposing groups will rise up against the government has resulted in a constitution that gives the president a great deal of control over the way the country is run. At the same time, Muslim beliefs that dominate the nation's religious practices also play a role in setting the laws of the land.

EXECUTIVE BRANCH

Syria's government structure has executive, legislative, and judicial branches. However, power is not divided equally among the different branches of government.

The most powerful branch of Syria's government, the executive branch, is led by its president, Bashar al-Assad. The president serves seven-year terms, but, since opposition is not allowed, the president receives nearly 100 percent of the vote in referendum elections. The country also has a prime minister, Mohammad Naji al-Otari, who is appointed by the president. There are two vice presidents and three deputy prime ministers. The Council of Ministers makes up the president's cabinet. Bashar al-Assad and people appointed by him make most of the political and economic choices that impact Syria, such as placing taxes on goods brought into the country and controlling the country's banking system. The president can declare war, issue laws, and change the constitution. He also can appoint people to civil service positions and to jobs in the military.

LEGISLATIVE BRANCH

The legislative arm of the government is the People's Council. Before 1970, when it was renamed by Hafez al-Assad, it had been called the Parliament. Members are elected to four-year terms of office. While the president can issue laws, the laws must be ratified by the People's Council. The council of 250 members can also propose laws and approve the way Syria spends money through its national budget.

The majority of the People's Council members are from the Baath Party, but it does have members from outside the party. In a move in keeping with Bashar al-Assad's desire to keep government control out of the hands of a powerful, wealthy elite, at least 50 percent of council members must be workers and peasants.

Although it can ratify laws, in reality, Syria's People's Council has little power over laws that are initiated by the executive branch of government. Technically, council members are supposed to be able to offer alternative views to proposed policies and make changes to suggested laws. However, there

Members of the People's Council meet in 1995. The legislative branch of Syrian government, the Council exercises very limited political power.

HEALTH CARE

One of the services Syria's government provides to its people is health care. It is available in most of Syria's villages, although rural areas have fewer doctors than urban areas. In an attempt to bring medical specialists to poorer areas, Syria requires doctors, dentists, and pharmacists who do not intend to specialize to practice in rural areas for two years after finishing medical school.

In addition to public health care, private health care is also available for a fee. Private health care services are viewed by some to be of higher quality than the services provided by the government. Some doctors have both a government and a private practice, to make up for their low government salaries. Government workers and their families have the best of both worlds—they can be partly or fully reimbursed for visits to private doctors as well as use the public health care system.

The health of children in Syria sometimes suffers due to poverty and poor nutrition, but more than 90 percent have been immunized against measles. The country's infant mortality rate of 31.67 deaths per 1,000 live births is higher than the U.S. rate of 6.75, but it has been falling. The country's life expectancy rate is sixty-eight years for a man and almost seventy-one years for a woman.

Although health care in Syria has improved over the past twenty years, some Syrians prefer to be treated with traditional medicine, which involves cures made from plants and spices. For example, a bee sting is soothed with a piece of a garlic clove, and colds are treated with cinnamon, honey, and lemon.

is not much they can do once something is proposed by the president. Two members of the People's Council were arrested in 2001 when they offered suggestions for political reform.

JUDICIAL SYSTEM

Syria's judicial system is influenced by systems put in place throughout the country's history, with some of its traditions dating from the time of the Ottoman Empire. Islamic judicial processes also play a role in how the country's court system works.

Syria has separate secular and religious courts. Civil and criminal cases are heard in secular courts, while religious courts hear cases involving personal status, including matters relating to marriage and inheritance. Muslim issues are handled in a court that follows the sharia, or Muslim legal code. People of other religious faiths have personal and family issues settled in separate courts according to their religious background. This practice dates back to the religious tolerance of the Umayyads and the time of the Ottoman Empire, when members of non-Muslim religious groups were given an exemption from following Muslim law.

In the secular courts, cases of lesser offenses are first tried in front of a judge in the Courts of Peace, or Courts of Conciliation. More serious civil or criminal cases are first heard in the Courts of First Instance. If the crime is severe enough that the punishment may be more than three years in prison, a criminal case can also be heard in a judicial inquest court called the Court of Assize. Decisions made in the lower courts can be appealed to an appeals court. Verdicts made by an appeals court can be nullified by a panel of three judges in the Court of Cassation.

The five members of the Supreme Constitutional Court, who are appointed by the president to four-year terms, rule on the constitutionality of laws. Judges for other courts are appointed and dismissed by the High Judicial Council. Cases of national security can be heard in state security courts. These courts operate under the government's state of emergency, rather than ordinary law, and do not give defendants the same constitutional rights of other courts.

PROVINCES

In addition to the executive, legislative, and judicial branches of the national government, Syrians also follow local laws. Syria is a republic that is divided into fourteen provinces. Each province is led by an appointed governor and an elected provincial council. The capital city of Damascus is administered by its own governor.

The governors of the provinces are appointed by Syria's Ministry of the Interior. They are in control of the government of their region and report to the president. The districts, counties, and villages of Syria also have locally elected officials.

The local governments are funded by Syria's central government. Syria's government is very centralized, and local leaders often look to the central government for guidance rather than making independent decisions. However, at times, project decisions are made locally. In Damascus, for example, the local government put a regional program in place to slow urban sprawl and preserve open land.

POLITICAL PARTIES

Most of the officials elected to government positions belong to a political party that is part of the National Progressive Front, a group of political parties led by the Baath Party. Syria's president is the secretary general of the country's Baath Party and is also the leader of the National Progressive Front. In addition to the Baath Party, other political parties in the National Progressive Front include the Socialist Unionist Democratic Party, the Syrian Communist Party, the Unionist Socialist Party, the Arab Socialist Party, the Arab Socialist Unionist Movement, the Syrian Arab Socialist Party, and the Syrian Social National Party. Of the 250 seats in Syria's People's Council, 167 are reserved for members of these parties. The remaining council members are independent. The country's constitution stipulates that the Baath Party have the most members on the council.

The country's government structure allows the Baath political party, whose members have led Syria since 1963, to have much influence over the country. It has built a power base of military members and is also popular among religious minorities and peasant farmers. It has gained popularity among the poor by giving them a voice in government.

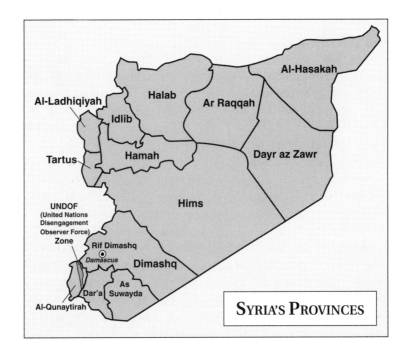

At the local level, 60 to 70 percent of positions must be filled by peasants, workers, and craftsmen.

The Baath Party has maintained a powerful position in Syrian society because of the control the government maintains over the nation's industries and economy. Membership in the Baath Party is often a condition of advancing in the military or getting a government job. Baath Party members are prominent in the country's government, and government officials are the ones who appoint people to civil service jobs and partition agricultural land to farmers. Because the government controls a large bureaucracy, it has created a supportive group of people who are dependent on the Baath Party for their livelihood.

MILITARY

Moving up in the military is often seen as a way of advancing in Syria's political system. Hafez al-Assad rose through the ranks as an air force officer, and his son Bashar also served in the military while he was being groomed as president. As president, Bashar al-Assad is now the commander in chief of the armed forces, which includes four hundred thousand troops in the army and air force. About twenty thousand of these soldiers are stationed in Lebanon. Because other Middle Eastern nations rely on Syria to maintain pressure on Israel, and pay it to do so, Syria has one of the largest military forces in the Middle East.

It is costly to maintain such a large military, and Syria spends a sizeable portion of its national budget on defense. In 2002, it was estimated that Syria spent $800 million on its military. In addition to paying for military personnel, the country must pay for tanks, airplanes, and other military equipment.

Serving in the military is compulsory for young men in Syria. Men must serve in the military for thirty months after they reach age eighteen. Women can also volunteer to serve. There are ways for men to get around the mandatory military service, however. A man who does not want to serve can pay a sum of money, usually thousands of dollars, to avoid military service. This fee is too expensive for many Syrians to pay, though.

In addition to its army and air force, Syria also has military and intelligence units that are controlled by Bashar al-Assad

Female soldiers march during a 1958 parade. Service in Syria's army is compulsory for men and voluntary for women.

and are used to keep order within Syria. These include the Presidential Guard, which maintains security around the Presidential Palace in Damascus. Most of the members of these units are either from the same Muslim sect as Bashar al-Assad, the Alawi, or are from the northwest region of the country. Bashar al-Assad maintains, as his father did before him, that political freedom in Syria needs to be tightly controlled to protect the country. Syria has been under a state of emergency since 1963, and the government says this state of emergency is warranted because the country is at war with Israel.

ECONOMY

The expense of maintaining its military forces takes its toll on Syria's economy, which is growing more slowly than the country's population. Because Syria is not as rich in oil reserves as other nations in the Middle East, it must rely on aid from wealthier countries to support its economy. The loans and foreign aid Syria receives are often spent on its army and air force rather than on programs for its citizens or improvements in infrastructure, such as road building. The political decisions of Syria's leaders have a direct impact on the country's economy as well. For instance, the United States has curbed investment in Syria because of the country's support of terrorist groups.

Syria's leaders keep a tight hold on the country's economy, as the government controls prices, trade, and the foreign exchange rate. Government control of the nation's industries dates to the Socialist policies of the Baath Party in the 1960s. This allowed the government to take the wealth of an upper class and distribute it more equally to Syria's people. Today about a third of Syria's industries are controlled by the state.

State control of industry gives the government a great deal of influence over who gets appointed to jobs in these areas. Syria's Baathist government has input into who is appointed to government-sponsored jobs and has traditionally provided its supporters with civil service positions. Qualifications for a government-supported job in Syria often rest on one's political allegiance or ethnic background rather than knowledge or skill in a particular area. This leads to some areas being poorly administered, with little room for independent decision making. "Most local and low-level staff have little expertise or training in administration, leading to very low efficiency," notes the Programme on Governance in the Arab Region, sponsored by the United Nations Development Programme's Regional Bureau for Arab States. "High-ranking officials tend to take control of administration, frequently through personal connections and affiliations. Thus, most governmental operations tend to be very top-down in their approach."[2]

Syria's strict control of prices and trade with other countries has curbed the growth of the country's economy, as government control has discouraged competition and innovation and has hurt industrial growth. The nation is heavily in debt.

Syria's economy also suffered when Saddam Hussein's Iraqi government fell in 2003 to U.S. forces. Iraq had been selling oil cheaply to Syria, which processed and sold it, in return for the use of Syria's ports. The loss of that income hurt the country. "We depend on oil sales and agriculture, which means everything is about petroleum prices and the weather,"[3] said Samir Seifan, managing director of Economic Business Consultants in Damascus.

FREEDOM OF SPEECH

The workforce and industry are not the only areas where Syria's government exerts its power. The freedom to express one's ideas and opinions, if they are different from ideas supported by the government, is limited in Syria. For example, the government has placed tight limits on freedom of speech.

SYRIA'S INDUSTRIES

The petroleum, mining, and textile manufacturing industries provide jobs for about 32 percent of Syria's workforce. Rug weaving has been a Syrian tradition, and the nation continues to produce high-quality textiles which it exports to other nations. The traditional dried fruit packing industry also remains an important part of Syria's economy.

Agriculture also is a dominant part of Syria's economy, and 32 percent of the country's workforce has jobs in agriculture. A third of Syria's land can be used for farming. Farmers grow wheat, barley, and cotton, in addition to chickpeas, olives, lentils, and sugar beets. Farmers raise sheep, chickens, and cattle, which are used to provide both beef and milk. Raw cotton, fruits, and grains are among Syria's major exports. Most farmers own their own farms. However, the government controls the markets where their goods are sold and the transportation system used to get the goods to market.

Most of Syria's agricultural workers depend on rainfall to grow their crops and feed their animals. In a country where drought can be severe, the dependence on rainfall hurts the country's agricultural output, as well as the economy as a whole. Irrigation is not widespread, which holds the agricultural economy back. Eighty percent of Syria's farmers depend on rain rather than irrigation to water their crops, and a severe drought in the late 1990s lowered Syria's agricultural output. For example, grain production was down nearly 40 percent.

Like these garment workers, a large percentage of Syria's labor force works in textile manufacturing.

When President Hafez al-Assad was in power, the government controlled the information that Syrians received, including the content of newspaper articles and television broadcasts and access to foreign newspapers. The president limited information because he did not want Syrians to receive information or share opinions that were critical of the way the government was running the country. The government also wanted to limit Syrians' exposure to ideas and opinions other than those advocated by the government. For example, when Internet service was introduced in Syria, it was made available only to a select number of people. Syria began providing Internet services for a $50 monthly fee in 1999. However, e-mail services were provided only for people with special occupations such as doctors, journalists, and lawyers. President Bashar al-Assad pledged to increase Internet access in 2000, but access is still curtailed, according to the U.S. Department of State.

National security is often given as the reason for suppresing information to the Syrian people. The nation's newspapers and magazines cannot publish unofficial information about the strength of Syria's army, or the weapons or the equipment it uses. Syria's government contends that the country's continuing conflict with Israel gives the government a reason to censor the information delivered to the nation's people. They say the chance that stories could be planted in the Syrian press by Israel gives them the right to closely watch what is printed in the nation's newspapers and broadcast on television.

When Bashar al-Assad came to power in 2000, the country loosened its press censorship policies a bit in order to gain more widespread support for the new leader. Syrians were allowed to install satellite dishes that received television programs from other nations. New newspapers were allowed to be published, and foreign newspapers became more readily available. More Internet access was allowed.

In 2000, the weekly newspaper *Al-Domari* broke new ground in Syria when it began publishing satirical articles that criticized the government. The newspaper still must operate within the guidelines of the Baath Party, however. The newspaper is distributed by an official government distributor, which means that the government can limit its audience, and the newspaper's editors do not have control over where it is read. The government also controls which companies can advertise in the paper, and a state-owned Arab Advertising Institution gets to keep more than a quarter of the money that comes into the paper for advertising. Another fee is paid to the state distributors.

If it wants to continue to publish, the newspaper must be careful not to offend people who are in favor with the government. "We are like someone in the bathroom who finds the water is hot one minute and cold the next," said *Al-Domari* editor and cartoonist Ali Farzat. "We are forced to talk in

Although the government's control of the content of popular media has eased in recent years, censorship of information remains a fact of daily life in Syria.

symbolic terms. Some months we can't talk about certain ministers and some social issues, but we must expect such things."[4]

REFORMS

Although there are people who would like to see Syria's position on freedom of speech reformed, the fear of civil war between the country's various ethnic groups keeps tight government controls in place. Changes in Syria's policies must come from top government officials, because citizens risk arrest and jail if they speak out in a way that criticizes the government. Although Syrians have a say in who gets elected to local government positions, they do not really have the opportunity to change the country's top leadership. In national elections in which Bashar al-Assad and his father were elected, they typically garnered close to 100 percent of votes.

Syria's economy is not prospering under the present system, and in order to stem discontent, Bashar al-Assad has promised to implement some changes in a few areas of the nation's government. When he swore in a new cabinet in 2003, Bashar al-Assad said administrative and economic reform were the priorities of the administration: "An even-handed judiciary is the basis for the state of law."[5] He also showed support for judicial reform by abolishing some unfair courts that operated under the guise of national security.

Bashar al-Assad faces a difficult task if he wishes to make significant changes in the way the country operates, however. Those that benefit from the way the government and economy are presently run, including influential members of the Baath Party and some of his relatives, would lose out if private industry prevailed over government-run businesses.

DAILY LIFE

5

The day-to-day life of people in Syria is less influenced by the government than it is by centuries-old traditions and well-ingrained values. The way people behave toward one another, the work that they do, and the homes that they live in reflect ways of life that go back centuries. Religious practices, family life, and women's roles in society are often based on traditional beliefs. Syria's people mostly live in communities with others who share similar backgrounds, language, and religious beliefs. For example, Bedouins roam the southern part of the country or inhabit small villages, and some Christian groups still speak Aramaic, the language Jesus spoke.

While Syria's people rely heavily on tradition to guide them in their daily life, the country is not isolated from change. As more information enters Syria through television, the Internet, and some foreign newspapers and magazines, people are introduced to new ideas. There are hints of modernization in areas such as clothing styles, and the country's stores carry electronics as well as traditional handicrafts and embroidery.

In a nation that has been inhabited for thousands of years, the old and the new are often mingled. In the capital of Damascus, homes built when Syria was ruled by the Ottoman Empire take on a new role as restaurants and trendy coffee shops. In the bazaars, or souks, people barter for fresh meat and produce as they have for centuries, but elsewhere in the city the streets are jammed with late-model cars.

INHABITANTS

The vast majority of the people living in Syria are Arabs, who are generally defined as people who speak Arabic. In fact, Arabs make up 90 percent of Syria's population of 17.6 million. However, all Arabs do not follow the same customs or have the same lifestyle. Within Syria's Arabic community there are distinct differences between ethnic and religious groups, and between those who live in urban and rural areas.

57

THE KURDS

The Kurds that live in Syria's northeast and Aleppo areas, as well as in neighborhoods in Damascus, are part of an ethnic group that reaches across several countries in the Middle East. The Kurdish community overlaps the borders of Turkey, Iraq, and Iran, as well as Syria. The Kurds, who are Sunni Muslims but are not Arabs, had hoped to receive an ethnic homeland of Kurdistan after World War I, but the country was not created.

The Kurds have met with conflict in Turkey and Iraq, as the governments of those countries put down Kurdish revolts. After Saddam Hussein's Iraqi government was toppled in 2003, the Kurds gained a new degree of freedom and status in that country as they allied themselves with the United States against Hussein. The Kurds in Syria have not suffered armed conflict with the government, but they do not enjoy political freedom.

Although Kurds make up 9 percent of Syria's population, their culture is not recognized by Syria's government. It is illegal to speak the Kurdish language in Syria's schools, and the Kurds cannot publish a newspaper in their own language. Kurdish leaders have asked the Syrian government to allow it

more cultural freedom, and human rights groups have asked that Syria's government give more economic aid to the poor northeastern provinces where most of Syria's Kurds live.

Kurds like these women constitute 9 percent of Syria's population, but the Syrian government does not recognize their culture.

Arabs can be Muslim, Christian, or an offshoot of those religions. They may live in cities, villages, or the desert.

While Arabs live in all areas of the country, members of Syria's ethnic and religious groups are usually concentrated in one or two areas. A person's style of dress, housing, etiquette, and view of other cultures is usually based on what is done within the region or religious community that person lives in. The country's largest ethnic minority, the Kurds, generally inhabit the Jezira region of northeastern Syria. Other minority groups in Syria include Armenians, Circassians, and Turkomans. Millions of Armenians fled to Syria during

World War I when they were being persecuted in Turkey. They settled mainly in the cities of Aleppo, Dayr az Zawr, and Al-Hasakah. Circassians, who are non-Arab Muslims, came to Syria from the Russian Caucasus region in the nineteenth and twentieth centuries. Some Turkish-speaking people, as well as those who speak Aramaic, also live in Syria. Several hundred thousand Palestinians live in Syria as well, mainly in the Damascus area.

RELIGION

The people who live in Syria are predominantly Muslim. About 90 percent of Syrians belong to the Muslim religion. Although Syria does not have an official state religion, religious beliefs heavily influence the daily lives of many Syrians. While Hafez al-Assad was in power, he ordered the building of hundreds of mosques. Shops are generally closed on Fridays, the Muslim day of rest. Muslim prayer leaders deliver sermons on Fridays, as worshippers crowd mosques. The call to prayer is proclaimed from the minarets of the mosques five times a day. Muslims pray in a prostrate position facing the mosques, or they lay face down on a prayer mat to pray wherever they happen to be at the time of prayer.

The Sunni sect is the predominant Muslim sect in Syria, almost three-quarters of the Muslim population. Forty percent of Sunni Muslims live in cities, mainly Syria's larger ones, while the rest live in the country's villages and desert region. Hafez al-Assad's decision to increase the number of mosques in the nation was based in part on a desire to please Sunni Muslims, who often looked down on his religious sect, the Alawi.

Twelve percent of Syria's Muslims are Alawis. The Alawis are an offshoot of Shia Islam. They believe that Ali, the son-in-law of the prophet Muhammad, is divine. People who belong to other Muslim sects consider this belief to be heretical, and do not consider the Alawis to be truly Muslim. Members of the Alawi sect live mainly in the Latakia area in northwestern Syria, in rural areas along the Mediterranean coast, and in the mountains.

Christians make up about 10 percent of Syria's population. Most Christians are Arab and belong to the Greek Orthodox or Greek Catholic Church. There are also members of the Armenian Orthodox Church in Syria, and in the city of Aleppo there is a close-knit Armenian Catholic population. Other Christian groups in Syria include the Syrian Catholic Church, the Roman Catholic Church, and the Syrian Orthodox Church, whose members celebrate Mass in the Aramaic language. Some of Syria's Christians belong to the Protestant and Anglican churches, whose missionaries came to Syria in the 1800s. Christians generally live in the coastal mountain region, usually near cities such as Damascus, Aleppo, Hamah, and Latakia.

About 3 percent of Syria's people are members of the Druze religious community. The religion is related to Islam, but many Muslims do not recognize the Druze religion as Muslim because of their worship of the Muslim leader al-Hakim, who disappeared in 1021. The Druze believe that God incarnated himself in al-Hakim and that he will return to the world to usher in a new golden age. The Druze marry within their faith and are secretive about their religious practices. They do not admit new members to their faith. They generally live in the Jabal al-Arab mountains in the south. (The Druze had lived in the mountains of Lebanon until the 1860s, when many migrated to Syria after a clash with Ma-

Christians like this Greek Orthodox priest are a minority in Syria, comprising only about 10 percent of the country's population.

ronite Christians in which thousands of the Maronites were killed by the Druze.)

Other religious groups in Syria include the Ismailis, a sect of the Shia branch of Islam who live between Homs and Aleppo. There is also a small Jewish community in Syria, mainly in the Damascus and Aleppo areas, as well as Kurdish-speaking tribes that follow the Yazidi religion, which includes elements of Judaism, Christianity, and Islam. Yazidis believe in God as creator and worship Malak Taus, or Peacock Angel, as their chief divine figure. About fifteen thousand Yazidis live in Syria near the Iraqi border.

LANGUAGE

Most people in Syria speak Arabic, which is the official language of the country. It developed from the ancient languages of the Middle East and is a Semitic language, as are Hebrew, Aramaic, and Syriac.

There are several forms of Arabic, including Classical Arabic, Modern Standard Arabic, and Syrian Arabic. Classical Arabic is the language of the Koran, which gives the language a special significance to all Muslims. "Because Classical Arabic is the language of the Quran [Koran] and is regarded literally as the language of God, Arabs almost unanimously believe that the Arabic language is their greatest historical legacy,"[6] writes Thomas Collelo in *Syria: A Country Study*. The formal language is Modern Standard Arabic, the written form of the language that is universal throughout the Arab world. The commonly spoken dialect in Syria is Syrian Arabic. Although almost all Arabs understand Modern Standard Arabic, different forms of Arabic are spoken in various villages and by different social classes throughout the Middle East. These can be quite different from the standard version, and it is sometimes hard for two Arabic speakers of different dialects to understand what the other is trying to say. Even within Syria there are slightly different dialects in various regions of the country.

Arabic is a flowery, emotional language given to overstatement and repetition. An emphatic greeting, such as "peace be to you," or "hello," is usually accompanied by a handshake. The response is likely to be a more emphatic greeting, such as "to you be peace also," or "hello and welcome," and perhaps a hug and a kiss on the cheeks.

The French rule over Syria in the early part of the 1900s made the French language part of the country's fabric. French is still widely understood in Syrian cities, as is English. In smaller cities and rural areas, people speak their own Arabic dialect or another language used by their ethnic group. Ethnic languages such as Kurdish, Armenian, Aramaic, and Circassian are all spoken in parts of Syria.

FAMILY LIFE

The various ethnic and religious groups may speak different languages and have distinct beliefs, but all have one thing in common: They place a high priority on family. Syrians view the ideal household as having three generations: grandparents, their single and married children, and grandchildren. After marriage a couple lives with the husband's relatives rather than setting up a separate household. This family structure is more common in rural villages than in Syria's urban areas, where fewer members of an extended family live in the same household.

Marriages are almost always within a person's ethnic or religious group. They are often arranged, especially in rural areas and villages, as well as among the Bedouin tribes. People usually marry another person from the same social class. Even when a marriage is not arranged, the parents of the couple must agree to the marriage.

With family life such an important part of society, it is not surprising that Syrians also place a high value on children. The majority of Syria's population is young, with 60 percent of its people under age twenty. It is such an honor to have a child in Syria that the parents are often identified by the name of their son, and they will often replace their own name with "mother of" or "father of" in front of the child's name. If the family only has daughters, the mother often adds the name of the oldest girl to her name.

The close family ties that evolve from marrying within one's ethnic group and social class mean that Syrians are extremely loyal to their relatives. In business dealings, they prefer to work with a member of their extended family rather than go outside the family group. Businesses are often run by people who are related to each other. It can be difficult for an ambitious Syrian to get ahead without family connections.

ATTITUDES TOWARD WOMEN

Family life is especially important to Syrian women. Married women spend most of their time working at home, shopping for their family, and raising their children. Fewer than 10 percent of women work outside the home.

Women technically have the same rights as men in Syria. However, they are still viewed as needing protection from their male relatives from men who are not related to them. Women are expected to behave modestly. In public, they generally socialize only with other groups of women and do not converse with men, except for their husbands. Men gather in public to talk, to drink tea or coffee, or to smoke water pipes, while women typically go out to a social event only if they are with their families or husbands. Most of their socializing is done at home with other relatives.

A small number of Syrian women, however, are taking on roles usually reserved for men, becoming active in business or politics in spite of the social customs that emphasize a more traditional role for women. There have been female cabinet ministers, and women have also been elected to other government posts. One Syrian businesswoman, Khulud Halaby, sees women in Syria balancing their lives between their rights as Syrian citizens and their role as women in Syrian culture. "Syrian women enjoy legal rights, the very same as men, without any discrimination," she says. "There remains however some family and social restrictions which vary in strength with the social status, and can be extremist

The unhappiness of this bride newly married to a husband of her parents' choice is evident in this photo. Arranged marriages are a common practice throughout Syria.

in certain cases. The target today is to encourage these women to develop their skills and broaden their horizons without necessarily breaking any social or family bonds."[7]

EDUCATION

Education is seen as the most likely way for a Syrian woman to broaden her options. Girls have the same right to education as boys in Syria, and the country's government is beginning to encourage girls to continue their education past the basic, mandatory education that ends at age twelve. Syria Live, an English-language Web site offering news and information on Syria, is upbeat about the strides the country has made in education: "Undoubtedly, Syria has made significant progress over the last three decades as regards to compulsory education and the spreading thereof. Education has changed from dictation to education, whereas equality and equal opportunities have been ensured for girls in all stages."[8]

Syrian women enjoy the same educational opportunities as men. Recent reforms have significantly improved the country's education system.

In the past, Syria's educational system had not done a good job of educating its citizens, and this has hurt the nation's economy. However, it has been making strides in teaching its people to read and write. The country has a literacy rate of 90 percent for males and 64 percent for females.

Students begin attending school at age six and are required to attend classes through age twelve. They must at-

tend six years of primary school, followed by three years of intermediate school. Although most children go to primary and intermediate school, less than half go on to high school.

After ninth grade, students take a test to see if they qualify for an Intermediate Level Diploma. Students who go on spend three years in secondary school, from age fifteen to eighteen, and attend either a general or a technical school. After a year of introductory courses, students take classes based on their interests and abilities. Students at a general secondary school will concentrate on literary or scientific classes, while students at a technical secondary school will study industrial or commercial courses. Those who qualify for higher education, which is financed by the government, may attend a university or receive technical training. Students at a technical school may study agriculture, engineering, or teacher training. Students attending a university can earn a bachelor's degree and go on to earn a master's or doctorate degree in fields such as medicine, law, or science. Syria has universities in Damascus, Aleppo, Latakia, and Homs, and also has vocational and agricultural schools. Since the government pays for higher education, classes are large. Some Syrian students go abroad to study.

MAKING A LIVING

Education and training often determine the type of job a person will have. In Syria, the jobs people take also depend on the economic situation of their region, as well as family influence. In small villages, agriculture is likely to be the main occupation of the inhabitants. Men traditionally work in fields or tend to herds of animals, while women are in charge of children and the house.

Syria has an elite upper class as well as people who live in poverty, but the division between rich and poor is not as noticeable as in some countries. However, the salaries are generally not high, and some people must work two or three jobs to earn enough income to support their families. Syria's middle class is strongest in the larger cities where jobs can revolve around the petroleum or textile industries. The best-paying jobs generally go to people with government connections and to members of the Baath Party.

While some Syrians earn degrees as doctors and engineers, others continue to follow more traditional ways of life handed down to them by their ancestors. The Bedouin people were traditionally nomadic herders who followed their flocks. While some Bedouin have settled permanently in villages and go outside the village to tend their flocks, others are seminomadic and only live in the villages part of the year. The free-roaming Bedouin lifestyle of hunting, herding animals, and moving with the flocks is generally respected in Syrian society. However, some Syrians do consider the Bedouins to be inferior.

HOUSING

More and more Bedouins are being encouraged to settle in villages by Syria's government. Disputes over grazing land and water rights often arise between tribes in the desert and settlement helps the government to have more control over these issues. They had traditionally lived in tents in the desert, homes which could be set up and then easily taken down when the need to move arose. Those that have settled in villages may live in mud-brick homes shaped like beehives. These homes protect them from the extreme heat and the cold of the desert. An extended family may live in several beehive-shaped buildings.

Other Syrians live in small villages, where their style of home is often dictated by the terrain. A rural home may have a grape arbor over the roof to keep the house cool during the summer, while other homes have flat roofs.

About half of Syria's people live in cities, where neighborhoods are traditionally populated with people who follow the same religion or share the same background, but the growth of suburbs has stunted this tradition somewhat. The cities still have ancient quarters with a market and small shops as a focal point. Syria's cities are crowded, and only the wealthiest can afford a single-family home. Most people own apartments and often have several generations under the same roof.

Syrians are quick to welcome visitors into their home, a tradition that dates back to the harsh life in the desert when being invited in for water and rest might mean the difference between life and death. A traveler is likely to be invited into the house and asked to share a cup of tea. Upon entering the house, a person takes his or her shoes off. The house may be separated into separate quarters for men and women, and may have pillows on the floor for sitting upon.

CLOTHING

Syrian people dress in a variety of styles, often according to their ethnic background or religious beliefs. In rural areas, women and men tend to dress in more traditional clothing, with women wearing decorated dresses and head scarves and men wearing head wraps and long robes with buttons on the front.

Clothing styles in the cities tend to follow more modern fashions. Women most commonly wear a modest dress or skirt, with a head scarf similar to those worn in rural areas. Another common piece of clothing for women is a colorful raincoat. However, there can be a wide variety of clothing preferences shown among Syrian women. Some dress in conservative dark colors, while others wear brightly colored dresses, heavy makeup, and earrings. Some may also dress as Europeans or Americans do, in jeans or pants, if their religious beliefs allow it. However, Syrians draw the line at Western-style

The government has established a number of villages with beehive-shaped huts to provide housing for Syria's Bedouin population.

HEAD COVERINGS

Although clothing styles in some Syrian cities are more Western than in other Middle Eastern countries, Muslim women in Syria often wear the *hijab*, or head scarf, in public to cover their hair. The covering is in keeping with the Koran's requirement that women behave modestly. The Koran does not specifiy the veil as a necessary covering, but Muslim women have worn the *hijab* for centuries.

The *hijab* and veil were originally worn by upper-class women, and clothing that covered the face, the head, and the body in a loose fashion became

part of Muslim culture to varying degrees. While some Middle Eastern governments dictate that women must wear a certain type of veil or body covering, there are no such rules in Syria. Women in Syria are free to choose the clothing that suits their taste, as well as their ethnic and religious background.

Wearing a hijab, *or head scarf, is a common practice among Muslim women in Syria.*

clothing that would expose bare legs or upper arms. Shorts and sleeveless shirts are generally not worn by women in Syria.

Men living in cities generally wear a wrapped cotton headdress and may wear a long robe as men do in rural areas. However, they may also wear Western-style jackets, sweaters, and pants. The different clothing styles worn by the people of Syria reflect the country's ties to a multicultural past, as well as the way its people are looking to fit in with the present.

FOOD

Syria's past is also evident in the dishes that are served at mealtime. Syrian food is similar to that of other countries in the Middle East and has been influenced by the many cultures that have occupied Syria. For example, a traditional Syrian pastry called *batlawa* is similar to the Greek pastry baklava. A desert custard called French *batlawa* dates from the time of the French mandate. Other food that is common both in Syria and the rest of the Middle East is hummus, a paste of chickpeas. Turkish coffee, showing the influence of the Ottoman Empire, is served after a meal.

Syrian food is often eaten with Syrian pita bread. The flat pocket bread can be stuffed with cheese, hummus, or a combination of meats and vegetables. Favorite dishes include a dish of ground lamb called kibbe. One of the ingredients in that dish, and a popular one in general in Syria, is *burghol*. It

A baker prepares Syrian pita bread, a pocket bread that is stuffed with meats, vegetables, cheese, or hummus.

is made from wheat that is steamed before being dried and ground.

Lemon juice, garlic, and ground sesame seeds are also used in cooking, with lemon juice, garlic, and fava beans being mixed together to create *fuul*. Olives, yogurt, and white cheese are commonly served as well. Eggplant, rice, and lamb are other popular foods. A special Bedouin dish is a whole-cooked lamb, served over rice and pine nuts. Lamb meat can also be mixed with lemon and olives to create a stew.

Food is usually eaten with the right hand and is usually grabbed with the hand or scooped up with a piece of bread rather than eaten with a fork or a spoon. Instead of sitting at a table, people may eat a meal while sitting on the ground.

Mealtime can be a relaxing social pastime for Syrians. In restaurants, food is usually

ordered for the entire group and served family style. At a special social event, Syrians can chat for hours over a leisurely
meal. In keeping with social rules that typically separate men
and women, some restaurants are for men only. However,
they have a separate family area set aside for women.

The segregated restaurants are one example of how customs influence daily life in Syria. Traditional clothing, foods, and housing styles are part of the comfortable rhythm of daily life. The Syrian lifestyle brings together the past and present, as an adherence to the religious convictions and societal values that have endured for centuries is combined with an awareness of the way Syria works today. Strong ties to the past make it challenging for Syrians to change their attitude toward things such as education or entering into a job or career that is not consistent with their family background. However, changes are occurring, as women become more visible in politics and business and as Syrians blend traditions with the needs of the country today.

6

ARTS AND ENTERTAINMENT

Syria's past also plays a prominent role in the country's arts and entertainment. Artisans practice crafts that have been honed over centuries, making expertly designed gold and silver jewelry, as well as leatherwork, woodwork, and hand-blown glass. The nation's entertainment is rooted in the past as well, as storytelling traditions, dances, and customs in celebration are passed on from generation to generation. Even the country's buildings, both those that are presently in use and the ruins that rise from the desert sand, offer a glimpse into the country's past.

While the past is kept alive through traditional crafts and customs, Syrians also turn to movies, television programs, and contemporary literature for entertainment. Syrian singers perform popular music, while dancers combine traditional and contemporary movements to create a vibrant style.

ARCHITECTURE

Syria's buildings display the influences in architecture that the country's inhabitants have had on the region. Grand Roman columns rise from the desert sand, curved Persian arches grace windows and doorways, and remnants of the thick walls of crusader castles still hover over the countryside. In Hamah, the waterwheels that were built in the Middle Ages continue to be part of the landscape along the Orontes River, and mosques in many Syrian cities are graced by Turkish-style minarets and domes.

The Umayyad Mosque in Damascus is a good example of how many cultures have shaped Syrian architecture. Standing near the mosque are intricately decorated columns, column bases, and arches that once graced the Roman Temple of Jupiter, which was built in the first and second centuries and once sat on the site now occupied by the mosque. The site also housed a Christian church dedicated to St. John the Baptist during the fourth century, and the mosque contains the Shrine of John the Baptist. Smaller columns and arches near the mosque are from the Byzantine period and were once part of a group of shops.

Work began on the mosque in the eighth century, and domes and minarets were added over the centuries. Each minaret shows the influence of the culture that dominated Syria at that time. The Minaret al-Gharbiye, built in 1488, shows Egyptian influence, while Ottoman and other influences can be seen in the Minaret of Jesus, where Muslims believe Jesus will come down from heaven to battle the Antichrist before the Last Judgment. The mosque is also decorated with mosaics by artists from Syria, Egypt, and Turkey.

One of the most architecturally influential and impressive mosques in the world, the Umayyad Mosque also influenced the way other mosques were constructed. Its features such as minarets and fountains became part of mosque architecture in other cities as well.

The arches, columns, and minarets of the Umayyad Mosque in Damascus are indicative of the many cultures that have shaped Syrian architecture.

ARCHAEOLOGY AND RUINS

Just as the styles of many nations can be seen in the architecture of the Umayyad Mosque, the remnants of past civilizations can be seen on the Syrian landscape. Syria has a wealth of archaeological sites that date to the dawn of civilization. Remnants of Roman cities, Byzantine churches, and crusader castles can be found, and are some of the things that make Syria such a special place. "Syria is a country in ruins," explains the Lonely Planet Worldguide on its Web site. "The place is full of them: wall-to-wall walls, cast-aside castles, teetering teatros and fallen-down fortresses. Syria has squirmed under the thumb of empire builders from Rome, Persia, Egypt, Turkey and Babylon, and every last one of them has left their architectural tag on the place."[9]

The dry climate in the country's desert region has preserved portions of the cities and buildings of Syria's past. Parts of these ancient cities have been unearthed by archaeologists and are housed in museums around the world, while other sections have been moved to museums in Syria. A two-thousand-year-old synagogue unearthed in the northeastern part of Syria was moved to the National Museum in Damascus in the 1930s. It had been so well preserved by the desert sand that its paintings still vibrantly depict scenes from Israelite history, including the crossing of the Red Sea and Abraham sacrificing a ram.

SCULPTURES

The many countries and cultures that have inhabited Syria also provide the nation with a rich palate of artwork. Sculptures that grace Syria's museums and galleries include Greek sculptures depicting gods and goddesses. Archaeologists have unearthed impressive sculptures from the Roman era in Palmyra. One of the sculptures on display in the museum at Palmyra was carved when the city was at its peak in the second century. The one-ton stone slab shows the seven-foot-tall image of a winged goddess standing on a sphere, holding a man's head.

More recent Syrian sculptors often studied abroad. In the first half of the 1900s, Syrian sculptor Fethi Mohammed used facial details to create lifelike human busts. In keeping with Muslim restrictions that prohibit portraying the human form, some Syrian sculptors such as Sadiq al Hassan produce geometric designs. Mohammed Mira works in several styles and is known for abstract metal structures.

FOLK ARTS

The prohibition of using the human form in artwork is also reflected in Syria's folk arts. Rather than showing scenes of daily life, artwork relies on intricate designs to emote feeling. Calligraphy is a highly prized art form and is often used for decorative purposes. The intricate patterns of mosaics are also popular.

Designs and patterns have been passed down through the centuries, and thousands of people re-create these designs

PALMYRA

To the northeast of Damascus, in a desert oasis, are the ruins of the city of Palmyra. The city in the middle of the desert was on a trade route between Eastern countries in Asia and Western countries in Europe and boasted a wealthy class of merchant citizens in the first centuries A.D.

The location of the city, on the border of several empires, gave the people of Palmyra a great deal of independence. The legendary queen Zenobia, who some sources say had her husband, the king, murdered, defeated Roman forces and went on to take over parts of Syria. Although the citizens and leaders of Palmyra did their best to outmaneuver the Romans in both politics and warfare, the Romans had enough by A.D. 271. The Romans overran the city, leaving it in shambles. Zenobia was taken to Rome as a prisoner.

Palmyra remained inhabited for a few hundred more years, a shadow of its once elegant self. The city was eventually abandoned during the 1400s, but remnants of its proud past still stand. Its ruins are one of Syria's major archaeological sites. The pale stone walls of its temples, statues of its former citizens, and monumental arch remain.

The ruins at Palmyra are a visible reminder of the grandeur of the once-thriving merchant city.

in Syria's handicraft industry. Ethnic groups specialize in expertly crafted gold and silver jewelry, brass bowls, hand-blown glass, and mosaic woodwork. The Bedouins craft jewelry, knives, and textiles, and the country's souks, or bazaars, are filled with leatherwork, copperware, and wood carvings made by the Syrian artisans.

Woven prayer rugs and carpets, traditional clothing, and a brocaded fabric called damask are also specialties of the country's artisans. The prayer rugs and carpets are made to be used locally as well as exported and sold to tourists. Silk, cotton, and linen textiles are also used by the weavers, and

These brass and silver wares are fine examples of the many handicrafts on sale in souks, or bazaars, across Syria.

damask has been a specialty of Damascus weavers since the Middle Ages.

LITERATURE

In addition to handing down artistic traditions from one generation to the next, Syrians also have handed down stories. Practicing the art of conversation is a popular pastime in general in Syria. The oral storytelling tradition, in the style of Arabian Nights, is especially prominent among nomadic groups such as the Bedouin.

The oral tradition has also lent itself to poetry, which plays an important role in Syrian literature. The poems' lyrical character was enhanced and revered as the tales were handed down through the centuries. *Al-Mu'allaqaat* is a centuries-old collection of Arab poetry, and in the tenth century classical Arab poets Al-Mutanabbi and Abu Firas al-Hamdani used poetry to express emotion and deliver their messages and observances. The usage of poetry as a means to convey ideas and feelings continued through the centuries. As Syrians worked toward independence in the first part of the twentieth century, poetry reading became a vehicle for expressing the need for a national identity.

The list of Syrian writers also goes back centuries. Posidonius of Apamea is an ancient Syrian writer, and the Koran, the Muslim holy book written in the seventh century, is a beautiful example of the Arab writing style. More recent writers include Mohammed Kurd Ali, a twentieth-century Syrian writer and professor from Damascus. He was the minister of education under the government that led Syria for a brief time before the French mandate, and his works include *The Treasures of Grandfathers*.

Contemporary authors include screenwriter and novelist Nihad Sirees, who writes television scripts and historical novels. His television series *The Silk Market* presents the culture of Aleppo. Some of today's most influential Syrian

RELAXING THROUGH CONVERSATION

Syrian men and women sometimes relax by simply enjoying the art of conversation. The Arabic language lends itself to turning articulate and clever phrases, and groups of men and women enjoy getting together to talk, and occasionally one-up each other with a well-turned phrase. When the weather permits it, Syrians gather in local parks to chat in groups of men or women while the children play. In keeping with Syrian customs, these groups are usually made up of only men or only women.

Syrian men gather to smoke water pipes and relax in coffeehouses. They may also meet at bathhouses, which date from the time of the Ottoman Empire. The tradition of meeting at bathhouses to share thoughts about today's world shows how Syria's people continue to blend the old with the new.

A group of Syrian men relaxes with their narghiles, or water pipes, in a Damascus cafe.

writers have left the country to seek a place where they are allowed greater freedom of expression. These include the poet Adunis, who lives in exile in Beirut and has advocated radical change in Arab life, as well as poet Ghada al-Samman.

DANCE AND MUSIC

The poetic expression of Syrian literature carries over to the songs of Syrian singers. Arab tunes blend with Western styles in Damascus, as both traditional and Western instruments are used to make music on the streets. Traditional music still plays a role in Syrian life, as classical instruments such as the guitarlike oud, the flute, and small drums are played. Groups of Bedouin men may chant as a belly dancer performs.

Another popular style of music in Syria uses more Western-style instruments. Orchestral instruments are played by a group, with an Arab-style lead singer and a chorus providing the lyrics. Popular Syrian singers include George Wassouf and veteran Farid Atrash. Singers Asala Nasri and Mayada Hinawi compete to be Syria's top female vocalist.

Modern dance groups are just beginning to emerge in Syria and are combining the styles of the country's folk dances with modern techniques. Dance groups in bright costumes perform onstage in Damascus, and an international folk dance festival is held at Busra. Ballet is also presented in Syria, and dance groups from schools in countries such as France perform in Syria.

MOVIES AND TELEVISION

Movies as well as cultural groups from other countries have made inroads in Syria. Damascus hosts an international film festival each year. Films by Arab filmmakers, such as director Ghassan Shmeit, are a major part of the festival, but films from more than forty nations, including France, Egypt, India, and Algeria, are included in the hundreds of movies shown at the event. Performers such as actor As'ad Fida and actress Salma al-Masri are some of the Arab stars who appear in movies at Syrian theaters.

Syrian television is influenced by both Arabic and Western shows. Syrians with satellite television can watch comedy shows from the United States, as well as dramas and cartoons such as *Scooby Doo.* They can also watch cricket games televised from India or Arab-made programs. They may

choose to tune in to a program directed by Samir Husein, an Arab television director with a series called *Silence Age*. Syrian television performers include Gina Eid, Dina Harun, and Zinati Kudsyeh.

Syria also has government-run television stations, and programs and movies on these channels must comply with government standards. After Bashar al-Assad came into power, the stations were granted some independence in the messages their shows presented, and some tackled political issues such as freedom of speech. Others satirized corruption in government, taking a wry look at people who inform the government of political activists. Another poked fun at Syrian ethnic groups by showing Syrians from different backgrounds arguing over what the national food should be, although each were offering slight variations of the same dish.

Some Syrian television shows have raised the ire of the country's neighbors in the Middle East. Shows such as *Knight Without a Horse* and *Al Shatat* have been accused of being anti-Israeli. These controversial shows often air during the Muslim holy month of Ramadan, which is a popular time for television viewing in Syria as Syrians relax in front of the television after a large evening meal.

Modern dance groups like this one that blend folk and modern dance techniques are just beginning to emerge in Syria.

SPORTS

Syrians also relax by watching and participating in sporting events. Soccer is a sport that enjoys worldwide popularity, and Syria is no exception. Children in Syria kick soccer balls in the streets of cities and villages, and the country has soccer leagues and a national soccer team. The Syrian team competes against other nations in the World Cup competition, although it is not usually a top-ranked team.

Syria also sends athletes to the Olympics, and at the Summer Olympics in 1996 Ghada Shouaa won a gold medal in the heptathlon. Her victory in the event, which involves hurdles, high jump, shot put, long jump, javelin, and 200 and 800 meter sprints, was the first gold medal for a Syrian in Olympic competition. She also won a gold medal in the heptathlon at the World Championships in 1995. Syria's other Olympic medal came in 1984, when Joe Atiyeh won the silver in wrestling.

Soccer is Syria's most popular sport. Here, a player from the Syrian national team challenges a player from the Lebanese team for control of the ball.

Shouaa's gold medal was notable for reasons other than being Syria's first. Women from predominantly Muslim countries sometimes face resistance when they decide to compete in sports. Shouaa is a Christian, so she did not face a cultural backlash for her athletic endeavors. Syrian women of the Muslim faith may compete in sports, although they cannot do so in front of men. Syrian women have had success in volleyball, badminton, and swimming at the Muslim Women's Games, in which all of the participants and spectators are women. Syria's female athletes have also competed in sports such as basketball at the Arab Games.

Syria's major cities boast sports arenas and training facilities for athletes, and there is a race-car track in Damascus. Syria has also hosted international sports events, including the Pan Arab Games in 1976 and 1992. In 1987 the country was the host of the Mediterranean Games.

FESTIVALS

While Syrians enjoy watching or competing in sports, it is a minor diversion for most Syrians. Syrian society places more emphasis on family and religion than competition, and the most important celebrations in Syria are held on the days of religious festivals.

The Muslim religious holidays are the days of the largest celebrations in Syria. The biggest of these is Eid al-Fitr, which celebrates the end of Ramadan, the Muslim month of fasting. People usually dress in new clothing for the celebration and gather together with friends and family members for a huge feast. In addition to eating large amounts of food, the celebration includes praying together and giving gifts. The date of the festival moves each year because the Muslim calendar is based on the lunar year of 354 days. The date of another feast, Eid al-Adah, also moves, and marks the day when Muslims should make the pilgrimage to Mecca.

Christians in Syria celebrate the religious holidays of Christmas and Easter with their families; however, there are no large community festivals associated with these holidays. A few decorations appear in store windows in December, but other decorations such as Christmas lights are rare.

National holidays in Syria also celebrate the country's emergence as an independent nation. These include Evacuation Day on April 17, which commemorates the French removal of its troops in 1946. May 6 is Martyr's Day, in honor of Arabs who died in the 1916 independence movement. Revolution Day is celebrated on March 8, marking the 1963 change in leadership that brought the Baath Party to power. Syrians also celebrate Correctionist Movement Day, on November 16, commemorating the government overthrow that brought Hafez al-Assad to power. The 1973 war with Israel is remembered each year on October 6, the anniversary date of the start of the war.

Syrian government holidays celebrate the nation's independence and the accomplishments of its more recent past, while its most important festivals honor the religious heritage of its people. As these days of celebration show, Syrian culture constantly blends the past with the present. The folk arts, dances, and architecture that have evolved over the centuries remain an integral part of the nation's culture, and exist side by side with newer forms of expression, such as

RAMADAN

One of the practices of the Muslim religion is to fast during the month of Ramadan, the ninth month of the Muslim lunar calendar. Because the lunar calendar is shorter than the solar calendar, Ramadan begins eleven days earlier each year under the solar calendar. Ramadan is held apart from other months because it was during the month of Ramadan that Muhammad received his first revelation.

During the Ramadan fast, Muslims do not eat, drink, or smoke during daylight hours. This is designed to emphasize the frailty of the human body and to allow the focus to be on God and spiritual values. It also helps Muslims identify with the poor. Special prayers and the recitation of the Koran further serve to emphasize the importance of God in Muslim life.

During the month of Ramadan, families typically eat a meal before sunrise, and at dusk have a light meal, which can be called breakfast because the family is breaking the fast they observed during the day. A later meal is eaten with family and friends, and often contains special dishes and desserts eaten only during Ramadan. The month ends with the Eid al-Fitr, or the Feast of the Breaking of the Fast, which includes special meals and gift giving and can last for several days.

television programs, movies, and modern songs and dance groups. Rather than forgetting their past, Syrians continue to make traditions part of their daily lives. This strong adherence to tradition gives the nation a deep sense of its heritage, yet can also make it difficult for changes to be made in a country that is firmly tied to its past.

A shopkeeper bulks up his stock of candy in preparation for Eid al-Fitr, the feast that concludes the monthlong fast of Ramadan.

7

CONTEMPORARY CHALLENGES

While Syria's festivals mark proud moments of the country's past, its future will depend on how it continues to face modern challenges. Syria must address both political and economic issues. Its population is growing, yet the standard of living is not rising as fast as the nation is growing. Its relationships with neighboring countries are tenuous, and its ongoing conflict with Israel makes its future peace precarious. The ruling Baath Party wields a great deal of power in the country, suppressing all who oppose it. The corruption of the government prevents the country's economy from improving, as those who benefit from the corrupt system insist on keeping it in place.

The challenges faced by Syria fall into two categories: international issues and internal struggles. The two are not completely separate. Action by other countries directly impacts the people of Syria, and the way Syria's government rules over its people impacts the way other nations view Syria.

CONFLICT WITH ISRAEL

The desire for pan-Arab unity, which has roots that date back to the time of Saladin, still drives politics in contemporary Syria. Syria is in favor of Arab control in the Middle East, and the creation of the nation of Israel in 1948 immediately provoked the ire of Syria and other Arab nations who saw the Israeli state as an invasion of Arab land. Israel and Syria have fought each other in wars in 1948, 1967, and 1973, and the conflict continues as Israel blames Syria for harboring the terrorists who have been setting off bombs in the country.

U.S. president Bill Clinton attempted to help the two countries come to an agreement during peace talks in the late 1990s, but the talks broke down in 2000. Syria insists that the return of the Golan Heights, lost to Israel during the 1967 war, be a condition of peace between the two countries. This has been unacceptable to Israel, which does not want Syria to control the strategically important piece of land. Before the area was overtaken by Israel, the Golan Heights provided Syria with a location from which to rain down bombs on Israel. Israel sees control of the Golan Heights as critical to preserving the safety of its country.

Israel also accuses Syria of harboring terrorist groups that organize attacks in Israel. Syria and Iran support the guerrilla group Hizballah, which is a bitter enemy of Israel. Syria has allowed terrorist groups to congregate on its land because of its hatred toward Israel, and because it receives money from other Arab nations for giving the terrorists a place to come together.

The Israelis, angered at the terrorist groups congregating so close to their border, retaliated. On October 5, 2003, Israel launched its first military strike deep inside Syria in thirty years. It bombed what it said was a terrorist training camp near Damascus. A few days earlier, a Palestinian suicide bombing attack in an Israeli restaurant killed nineteen people. The Islamic Jihad, a terrorist group, claimed to have caused the attack, and Israel blamed Syria because it said

A Syrian family clears a security checkpoint in the Golan Heights. Syria maintains that the return of the Golan Heights is a prerequisite for peace with Israel.

HIZBALLAH

Syria has been criticized by the United States for its links to Hizballah. The radical militia movement was formed in 1982 in response to Israel's occupation of southern Lebanon. Hizballah seeks to establish Islamic rule in Lebanon and has called for the destruction of Israel. In the early 1980s, Hizballah was responsible for kidnapping Westerners and bombing a U.S. Marine barracks. Three of its members are on the FBI's list of Most Wanted Terrorists for a 1985 airplane hijacking.

Hizballah has several thousand supporters and a few hundred terrorist operatives. The group continues to plan and carry out kidnappings and attacks against Israel. The guerrilla group gets the majority of its support from Syria and Iran. Syria provides Hizballah with guidance on military strategy and how to run its operation, while Iran provides it with money.

Syria allowed the group to work out of offices in Damascus. Syrian officials, however, said the offices of extremist Palestinian groups had been closed.

A few days after Israel's attack, Bashar al-Assad told a reporter that Syria did not harbor terrorist leaders. "They are not the leaders, just rank-and-file officials," he said. "We reject expulsion, for more than one reason, but first and foremost on principle. These individuals do not break Syrian laws . . . and, most importantly, they are not terrorists." [10] In his view, Syria was complying with the wishes of Western nations by forcing the leaders to move out of headquarters in Damascus.

WEAPONS AND TERRORISM CHARGES

Israel's strike against Syria was condoned by the United States. The United States has also been concerned about the strength of the weapons Syria has on hand and is worried that Syria possesses chemical weapons. Bashar al-Assad defended his country's weapons building, saying that it was necessary in order for Syria to defend itself from the weapons of its neighboring nations. "The Americans are demanding that Syria be free of Weapons of Mass Destruction, yet when we demand that the entire region be cleared of

these weapons, they oppose us," he said. "They place many demands but what concerns us here is whether the Americans demands can be reconciled with Syria's interests."[11]

Although Syria helped the United States stop the al-Qaeda terrorist network after the September 11, 2001, attacks, Syria is listed as a sponsor of terrorism by the U.S. State Department. This means that the United States limits economic aid and bans arms imports and exports to the country. Syria is highly dependent on aid from other countries, and a decrease in foreign aid will hurt the country's economy.

The United States' concerns include claims that Syria allows "infiltrators" to cross into Iraq from Syria at remote border-crossing points. These infiltrators were thought to be responsible for attacks on American soldiers in Iraq. Bashar al-Assad said that Syria cannot possibly control its long border with Iraq and noted that terrorists could cross into Iraq from other nations as well. "The situation in the entire region is extremely chaotic," he said. "Arms smuggling is rampant. Unknown individuals escape across borders. Naturally, the Americans call them terrorists, since, according to them, anyone could be a terrorist, or rather, any *Arab* could be a terrorist."[12]

The United States tried to send Syria a message to stop allowing anti-Israel militant groups to organize inside its borders

An Iraqi guard scans the horizon along the Syria/Iraq border, a stretch of land that provides an easy escape route for terrorists fleeing Iraq.

by imposing economic and diplomatic sanctions on the country. In late 2003, President George W. Bush signed the Syria Accountability Act to try to force Syria to stop support of terrorists in Damascus and to halt programs that develop biological and chemical weapons, as well as medium- and long-range missiles. "Syria needs to change course, change its behavior, stop harboring terrorists,"[13] said Scott McClellan, a spokesman for President George W. Bush's administration.

Under the sanctions, the United States has the option of restricting economic and diplomatic ties with Syria. If the country does not comply with the U.S. requests regarding weapons and terrorists, the nation would not be allowed to purchase equipment that could be used by the military, and there could be travel sanctions as well. Secretary of State Colin L. Powell visited Syria and tried to persuade Bashar al-Assad to move against terrorism, but the United States was not impressed with the steps taken by Syria. More pressure was the solution. "Syria is a government at war with the values of the civilized world and a violent threat to free nations and free men everywhere," said House Majority Leader Tom DeLay, after the Syria Accountability Act of 2003 was passed by the House of Representatives. "We'll send a clear message to President Assad and his fellow travelers along the axis of evil: The United States will not tolerate terrorism, its perpetrators, or its sponsors. All our warnings are not to be ignored."[14]

LEBANON

The accountability act addressed Syrian intervention in Lebanon as well, making the removal of Syrian troops in Lebanon a condition of the act. Syria is heavily influential in the affairs of its neighboring country of Lebanon, allowing weapons and money to flow into Lebanon across its border. Since 1976 it has kept thousands of troops in Lebanon, and refuses to take them out, fearing that if it does the area will be occupied by Israel. Israel also has troops in Lebanon, and the Syrian and Israeli troops have clashed there over the years.

One reason for the attacks in the area is a dispute over Sheba Farms, on the northern border of the Golan Heights. Syria claims the land is part of Lebanon and supports resistance in Lebanon against the Israelis because of the Israeli occupation of this land. Bashar al-Assad said the Lebanese state must be strong enough to replace Syrian forces before Syria will leave Lebanon. He claims that Syria is in the midst of a troop withdrawal but said that the timetable is something that Syria and Lebanon must determine. He does not want Israel, the United States, or any other nation to pressure him to remove troops. The matter, he says, is between Syria and Lebanon. "It's a Syrian-Lebanese matter and we don't discuss it with outsiders," he said. "We and the Lebanese will decide." [15]

STAGNANT ECONOMY

Syria's determination to act as it sees fit may hurt the country's economy if it leads to the United States exercising its option of placing trade restrictions on the country. Syria's economy has been stagnating. The goods produced by Syrian workers and the services provided by them have failed to keep up with the growth of the country's population, and limiting trade would weaken the already fragile state of Syria's economy.

The nation's economy showed signs of becoming more robust after foreign aid flowed into Syria following the Gulf War in 1991 and development projects were put in place. However, the nation's economy has responded slowly, and the country owes billions of dollars to foreign countries.

Syria's economy has also been hurt by its government-controlled policies on prices and trade. Syria is trying to remedy this by establishing firmer trade ties with the European Union nations. Syrian industries accustomed to having prices protected by the government may face increased competition, as agreements with European nations force Syria to lower its tariffs and allow foreign goods to come into the country at lower prices. Syria is opening up its banking business as well, as legislation in the early part of this century gave private banks the opportunity to open in Syria. The banks give businesses an alternative to government-run institutions. However, it will take years for the new banks to make a difference in the nation's economy.

Syria's economy also faces challenges from the weather. Productivity from agriculture and industry is low, as unstable weather hampers harvests and outdated equipment makes

In an effort to jumpstart its sluggish economy, Syria's government began to allow private banks like this one to operate in 2003.

it difficult for the country's manufacturers to compete. There are also disputes over water rights with neighboring countries that control the flow of rivers into Syria, lowering the amount of irrigated land.

Rather than spend significant amounts of money on roads or irrigation, Syria continues to funnel many of its resources into its armed forces. More than half of the country's annual budget is spent on the military, and its state of war with Israel makes it unlikely that military spending will decrease in the future.

Another reason for Syria's economic troubles is the government's tendency to position the economy to add to personal gain to those in favor rather than improving the country as a whole. Corruption within the nation's government also makes things run inefficiently, leading to repression for those who are not part of the government's inner circle. Payments must be made to certain officials before business deals are allowed to go through, and this trickles down to everyday life as a customs person expects a "tip" in order to expedite a claim. A lack of internal checks on corruption has led to a decay of Syria's economy.

POPULATION

At a time when Syria's economy is stagnating, its population is increasing rapidly, as in many countries in the Middle East. The population is increasing by more than 2 percent per year according to a 2003 estimate, with nearly 40 percent of the country's population under fifteen years old. This puts a strain on the country's resources and economy.

Syria's high population growth impacts the percentage of people that are able to find jobs in the country. The country's unemployment rate was estimated to be 20 percent in 2002. That means one of every five people in Syria was looking for a job. As its young population enters the workforce, the unemployment rate could become even more severe.

LACK OF POLITICAL FREEDOM

Syrians dissatisfied with the country's economy can voice concerns to local government leaders, but they will not be able to have a say in who rules the nation as president, as

★ ★ WATER WORRIES

Water is a precious commodity in Syria, and the country faces challenges in getting water to its people and croplands. The country's main water resources are far from its high-population centers, and rural areas suffer as water is diverted to cities for use by people and industries. In areas that had depended on the natural flow of a river for a water supply, the redirection of water leads to desertification as land that could once be cultivated becomes desert.

A growing population puts a strain on Syria's water supply, and cities such as Damascus have old water systems that exacerbate the problem. The old systems have a difficult time getting at enough water to satisfy the needs of the growing city, although Damascus is looking at updating its system by pumping water from Syria's coastal area to the city. Syria's water supply is also hampered by the fact that Turkey controls the headwaters of the Euphrates River and has a number of dam projects planned and in place that would provide water to southern Turkey but would withhold it from Syria.

Syria does not allow political opposition to its top leader. The country has been under martial law since 1963, when it declared a state of emergency because of conflict with Israel. Because the country is engaged in this ongoing conflict, its leaders justify their strict hold over the country by saying that it is necessary in order to protect Syria from aggression from its enemies.

Syria's people face severe reprimands if they unite in opposition to the government. In 1982, the Syrian army killed an estimated ten thousand people in Hamah when the Muslim Brotherhood, a group of Sunni Muslims headquartered there, openly opposed the way Hafez al-Assad was running the country and used violence to make their point. The United Nations Human Rights Committee has reported that Syria has committed human rights violations, including searching homes and detaining and killing people without a trial. Syria has military units that provide its president with intelligence information on people with opposing political views, giving him information on where opposition to his government may be growing.

Amnesty International has accused Syria of violating the civil rights of political dissidents like Riad Turk, jailed for seventeen years for challenging the government.

Lack of government opposition from the general public means that few can criticize the large government bureaucracy, and the jobs it gives to those who support it. It has been risky to speak out in opposition to Syria's government during the leadership of Bashar al-Assad and his father. The president's decisions and policies are not open for debate.

Bashar al-Assad has promised to bring both judicial and economic reform to Syria. However, this will not be an easy task to accomplish. Although the general public cannot vote him out of office, he faces tough opposition from Baathist party members and others who benefit from keeping Syria's economy the way it is. The government's special military and intelligence units are used to acting outside of the legal system. It will be a challenge for Bashar al-Assad to change the system of government that his father successfully used to maintain control over Syria.

Any chance Syria has of changing the way its government operates rests with the country's top leader, however. The United States and the United Nations can apply pressure to Syria to encourage it to denounce terrorism, get rid of corrupt government policies, and protect human rights, but the route that Syria takes while Bashar al-Assad is in control will ultimately depend on his decisions. While Syria has deep ties to its past and Arab roots, it is Bashar al-Assad's choices and political alliances that Syria will carry into the future.

FACTS ABOUT SYRIA

GOVERNMENT

Name: Syrian Arab Republic

Independence: April 17, 1946

Capital: Damascus

Government type: Republic, under military regime since March 1963

Administrative divisions: Fourteen provinces

Executive branch: Chief of state—President Bashar al-Assad; Vice Presidents Abd al-Halim ibn Said Khaddam and Muhammad Zuhayr Mashariqa; Head of government—Prime Minister Mohammad Naji al-Otari; Deputy Prime Ministers Lt. Gen. Mustafa Talas, Farouk al-Shara, and Dr. Muhammad al-Husayn; Cabinet—Council of Ministers appointed by the president

Legislative branch: People's Council with 250 seats; members are elected by popular vote to serve four-year terms.

Judicial branch: Supreme Constitutional Court—the president appoints justices who serve four-year terms; High Judicial Council; Court of Cassation; State Security Courts

GEOGRAPHY

Area: 71,504 square miles

Bordering countries: Iraq, Israel, Jordan, Lebanon, Turkey

Terrain: Primarily semiarid and desert plateau, narrow coastal plain, mountains in the west

Elevation extremes:

Lowest point: an unnamed location near Lake Tiberias, 700 feet

Highest point: Mount Hermon, 9,232 feet

Land use: Arable land: 26 percent

Permanent crops: 4 percent

Other: 70 percent

Natural hazards: Dust storms, sandstorms

Environmental issues: Deforestation, overgrazing, soil erosion, desertification, water pollution from raw sewage and petroleum refining wastes, inadequate potable water

PEOPLE

Population: 17.6 million (2002 est.)

Age structure:

0–14 years: 38.6 percent

15–64 years: 58.2 percent

65 years and over: 3.2 percent

Population growth rate: 2.45 percent

Birth rate: 29.54 births/1,000 population

Death rate: 5.04 deaths/1,000 population

Infant mortality rate:

Total: 31.67 deaths/1,000 live births

Life expectancy at birth: 69.39 years

Total fertility rate: 3.72 children born/woman

Ethnic groups:

Arab: 90.3 percent

Kurds, Armenians, and other: 9.7 percent

Religion: Sunni Muslim—74 percent; Alawi, Druze, and other Muslim sects—16 percent; Christian (various sects)—10 percent; Jewish—tiny communities in Damascus, Al Qamishli, and Aleppo

Official language: Arabic

Literacy: 76.9 percent

Labor force: 5.2 million

ECONOMY

Gross Domestic Product (GDP): Purchasing power parity—$59.4 billion (2002 est.)

GDP growth rate: 3.5 percent

GDP per capita: Purchasing power parity—$3,500

Population below poverty line: 15 to 25 percent

Inflation rate: 0.9 percent

Unemployment rate: 20 percent

Budget: Revenues—$6 billion; Expenditures—$7 billion, including capital expenditures of $3.6 billion

Industries: Petroleum, textiles, food processing, beverages, tobacco, phosphate rock mining

Agricultural production: Wheat, barley, cotton, lentils, chickpeas, olives, sugar beets, beef, mutton, eggs, poultry, milk

Exports: $6.2 billion (crude oil, petroleum products, fruits and vegetables, cotton fiber, clothing, meat, live animals)

Imports: Machinery and transport equipment, food and livestock, metal and metal products, chemicals and chemical products

Currency: Syrian pound—49.65 Syrian pounds per U.S. dollar

NOTES

CHAPTER 1: FROM SEA TO DESERT

1. Ivan Mannheim, *Syria and Lebanon Handbook.* Bath, England: Footprint Handbooks, 2001, p. 17.

CHAPTER 4: GOVERNMENT SYSTEM

2. United Nations Development Programme: Programme on Governance in the Arab Region: Syria: Decentralization, *Syria: Decentralization and Urban Management.* www.undp-pogar.org.

3. Quoted in Stephen J. Glain, "Economic Threats Seen Jeopardizing Syria's Reform Efforts," *Boston Globe Online*, July 17, 2003. www.boston.com.

4. Quoted in Andrew Hammond, "The State of Syria's Media: 'Damascus Spring' or Indian Summer?" *World Press Review Online*, January 3, 2002. www.worldpress.org.

5. Naharnet Newsdesk, "Assad Swears in Syria's Reform Cabinet," September, 22, 2003. www.naharnet.com.

CHAPTER 5: DAILY LIFE

6. Thomas Collelo, ed., *Syria: A Country Study.* Washington, DC: Library of Congress, Federal Research Division, 1988, p. 65.

7. Quoted in Arabic News, "Great Hopes Pinned on Syria's Women and Education Forum," February 1, 2003. www.arabicnews.com.

8. Syria Live, "Syria Adapts Her Vision on Education," www.syrialive.net.

CHAPTER 6: ARTS AND ENTERTAINMENT

9. Lonely Planet. www.lonelyplanet.com.

CHAPTER 7: CONTEMPORARY CHALLENGES

10. Quoted in George Semann and Ghassan Sharbal, "Interview: Syrian President Bashar al-Assad," *Al Hayat* (London), October 7, 2003. www.worldpress.org.

11. Quoted in Semann and Sharbal, "Interview: Syrian President Bashar al-Assad."

12. Quoted in Semann and Sharbal, "Interview: Syrian President Bashar al-Assad."

13. Quoted in Brian Knowlton, "House Panel Votes to Impose Sanctions on Syria," *New York Times Online*, October 8, 2003. www.nytimes.com.

14. Quoted in Stuart Roy, "DeLay: Syria Accountability Act a Clear Message; 'Our Warnings Will Not Be Ignored,'" U.S. Newswire, October 15, 2003. http://releases.usnewswire.com.

15. Quoted in Semann and Sharbal, "Interview: Syrian President Bashar al-Assad."

GLOSSARY

alliance: Being in close association with another nation to further common interests

annex: To bring together or unite

caliph: A religious leader

fundamentalism: A movement that strictly adheres to a literal interpretation of basic principles

mandate: Being given the authority to act; also authority given to a member of the League of Nations, an association of nations that preceded the United Nations, to establish a responsible government in a conquered territory

nomadic: To roam about from place to place, having no fixed residence

sanctions: Economic or military measures taken by one or more nations to punish another nation for violating international law

Semitic: Relating to a language family that includes Arabic, Hebrew, and Aramaic

steppe: A vast, treeless area of land

terrorist: A person who uses terror as a means of gaining control

CHRONOLOGY

4500–538 B.C.
Ancient civilizations such as the Sumerians, Canaanites, Phoenicians, Assyrians, Egyptians, Hittites, Aramaeans, and Palmyrians inhabit Greater Syria.

538 B.C.
The Persians expand their influence westward into Syria.

333 B.C.
The Greeks enter Syria and establish cities.

64 B.C.
The Roman Empire begins its extension into Syria.

A.D. 330
Syria becomes part of the Byzantine Empire.

661
The Muslim religion spreads in Syria, and the Umayyads make the nation part of their empire.

1096
The crusaders enter Syria, fortifying castles and military strongholds.

1516
Syria becomes part of the Ottoman Empire.

1918
Ottoman rule ends; Damascus is captured by Arab troops.

1920
After a brief period of independence, Syria comes under French control.

1946
The last French troops leave Syria on April 17; Syria becomes independent.

1947
The Baath Party is founded.

1958
Syria and Egypt join the United Arab Republic; Gamal Abdel Nasser, the Egyptian president, becomes the leader.

1961
Syria leaves the United Arab Republic.

1963
Baath Party takes control of the government.

1967
In the Six-Day War, the Israelis take the Golan Heights from Syria.

1970
Hafez al-Assad controls the Baath Party and the government.

1971
Hafez al-Assad becomes president of Syria.

1973
Syria and Egypt go to war with Israel.

1982
Thousands of people are killed in Hamah as Syria's military suppresses a revolt by the Muslim Brotherhood.

1983
Hafez al-Assad suffers a heart attack and faces a threat from his brother, Rifat, who wants to take over as Syria's leader.

1990
Syria sides with the U.S.-led coalition against Iraq.

1999
Syria and Israel begin discussing the future of the Golan Heights.

2000
Talks between Syria and Israel end with no agreement; Hafez al-Assad dies in June, and his son Bashar succeeds him.

2003
Israel launches its first military strike deep inside Syria in thirty years on October 5; Israel bombs a suspected terrorist training camp near Damascus; President George W. Bush signs the Syria Accountability Act.

FOR FURTHER READING

BOOKS

John Morrison, *Syria.* Philadelphia: Chelsea House, 2003. An overview of Syria in the context of Middle Eastern history.

Coleman South, *Culture Shock! Syria.* Portland, OR: Graphic Arts Center, 2000. An insightful look at what it is like to live in Syria.

Diane Stanley, *Saladin: Noble Prince of Islam.* HarperCollins, 2002. A colorful book that details Saladin's historic and heroic accomplishments.

WEB SITES

Syrian Arab News Agency (www.sana.org). News reports and information on Syria.

Syria Online (www.syriaonline.com). Information on Syria's entertainment scene and culture, as well as travel.

The World Factbook (www.cia.gov). Statistics and historical information on Syria and other countries.

WORKS CONSULTED

BOOKS

Andrew Beattie and Timothy Pepper, *Syria: The Rough Guide.* London: Rough Guides, 1998. A traveler's guide to Syria.

Cambridge Encyclopedia of the Middle East and North Africa. New York: Cambridge University Press, 1988. Details of the civilizations that have inhabited the Middle East and North Africa.

Thomas Collelo, ed., *Syria: A Country Study.* Washington, DC: Library of Congress, Federal Research Division, 1988. Part of a series of country studies, the book gives background material on Syria's history.

Michael Kort, *The Handbook of the Middle East.* Brookfield, CT: Twentyfirst Century Books, 2002. An overview of the geography, the economy, and the history of nations in the Middle East.

Ivan Mannheim, *Syria and Lebanon Handbook.* Bath, England: Footprint Handbooks, 2001. Provides information about places in Syria and Lebanon.

Ivan Mannheim and Dave Winter, *Jordan, Syria & Lebanon Handbook.* Bath, England: Footprint Handbooks, 1998. A detailed look at Syria's cities and regions, with sidebars and anecdotes on the country's lesser-known features.

Geoggrey Orens, ed., *The Muslim World.* New York: H.W. Wilson, 2003. A collection of articles and essays explaining Muslim beliefs.

Abdul Latif Tibawi, *A Modern History of Syria, Including Lebanon and Palestine.* New York: St. Martin's, 1969. An academic look at the government of Syria from the time of the Ottomans until just before the 1967 war with Israel.

Internet Sources

ABC News, "Israel Explains Why Syrian Base Was Empty," October 8, 2003. www.abcnews.com.

Arabic News, "Continued Wide Condemnation of the Israeli Attack Against Syria," October 7, 2003. www.arabicnews.com.

———, "Great Hopes Pinned on Syria's Women and Education Forum," February 1, 2003. www.arabicnews.com

Iason Athanasaidis, "Syria: Odd Man Out in a Tough Neighborhood," *Asia Times Online*, October 18, 2003. www.atimes.com.

Boston Globe editorial, "A Message to Syria," *Boston Globe Online*, October 8, 2003. www.boston.com.

Badih Chayban, "Lahoud Declares Outrage as House Passes Syria Accountability Act," *Daily Star,* October 18, 2003. www.dailystar.com.

Stephen J. Glain, "Economic Threats Seen Jeopardizing Syria's Reform Efforts," *Boston Globe Online*, July 17, 2003. www.boston.com.

Andrew Hammond, "The State of Syria's Media: 'Damascus Spring' or Indian Summer?" *World Press Review Online.* January 3, 2002. www.worldpress.org.

Brian Knowlton, "House Panel Votes to Impose Sanctions on Syria," *New York Times Online*, October 8, 2003. www.nytimes.com.

Neil MacFarquhar, "Resurgence of Islam Seen as Aiding Syria," *International Herald Tribune,* October 24, 2003. www.iht.com.

Naharnet Newsdesk, "Assad Swears in Syria's Reform Cabinet," September 22, 2003. www.naharnet.com.

Reuters, "U.S. Forces Clash with Group on Syrian Border," AT&T Worldnet Service, October 15, 2003. http://dailynews.att.net.

Stuart Roy, "DeLay: Syria Accountability Act a Clear Message; 'Our Warnings Will Not Be Ignored,'" U.S. Newswire, October

15, 2003. http://releases.usnewswire.com.

George Semann and Ghassan Sharbal, "Interview: Syrian President Bashar al-Assad," *Al Hayat* (London), October 7, 2003. www.worldpress.org.

Dan Williams and Dan Trotta, "Syria Vows to Fight If Israel Attacks," Reuters, October 8, 2003. www.reuters.co.uk.

Web Sites

ABC News (www.abcnews.com). Source for information on current events.

Arabic News (www.arabicnews.com). A collection of daily news stories written from an Arab perspective.

AT&T Worldnet Service Daily News (http://dailynews.att.net). A collection of the day's top news stories from world news organizations.

Biography Resource Center (http://galenet.galegroup.com). Background information on world leaders and celebrities.

Cultural Profiles Project (www.settlement.org). A collection of information on world cultures provided by Citizenship and Immigration Canada.

Iexplore (www.explore.com). A travel Web site offering a variety of information about visiting countries around the world.

Infoplease (www.infoplease.com). Historical and statistical information on Syria.

Lonely Planet (www.lonelyplanet.com). Lonely Planet's Worldguide provides information on Syria's history, geography, and customs, as well as current travel information.

Mondo Times (www.mondotimes.com). Listing of world newspapers.

Reuters (www.reuters.co.uk). An online source for international news.

Syria Live (www.syrialive.net). Tourism and business information, as well as news updates about Syria.

United Nations Development Programme (www.undp-pogar.org). United Nations program dedicated to promoting good governance practices.

U.S. Department of State (www.state.gov). Current and historical information, as well as statistics, on nations around the world.

VIDEO

Pilot Productions, *Syria, Jordan and Lebanon*, Oakland, CA: Lonely Planet, 1999.

INDEX

PICTURE CREDITS

ABOUT THE AUTHOR

Terri Dougherty is a freelance writer from Appleton, Wisconsin. In addition to nonfiction books for children, she also writes magazine and newspaper articles. A native of Black Creek, Wisconsin, Dougherty has also worked as a newspaper reporter and an editor. She enjoys traveling, soccer, and reading, as well as skiing and just having fun with her husband, Denis, and their three children—Kyle, Rachel, and Emily.